# Hazardous Waste

Look for these and other books in the Lucent Overview Series:

Abortion
Acid Rain
Adoption
Advertising
Alcoholism
Animal Rights
Artificial Organs
The Beginning of Writing
The Brain
Cancer
Censorship
Child Abuse
Children's Rights
Cities
The Collapse of the Soviet Union
Cults
Dealing with Death
Death Penalty
Democracy
Drug Abuse
Drugs and Sports
Drug Trafficking
Eating Disorders
Elections
Endangered Species
The End of Apartheid in South Africa
Energy Alternatives
Espionage
Ethnic Violence
Euthanasia
Extraterrestrial Life
Family Violence
Gangs
Garbage
Gay Rights
Genetic Engineering
The Greenhouse Effect
Gun Control
Hate Groups
Hazardous Waste
The Holocaust
Homeless Children

Homelessness
Illegal Immigration
Illiteracy
Immigration
Juvenile Crime
Medical Ethics
Memory
Mental Illness
Militias
Money
Ocean Pollution
Oil Spills
The Olympic Games
Organ Transplants
Ozone
The Palestinian-Israeli Accord
Pesticides
Police Brutality
Population
Poverty
Prisons
Rainforests
The Rebuilding of Bosnia
Recycling
The Reunification of Germany
Schools
School Violence
Smoking
Space Exploration
Special Effects in the Movies
Sports in America
Suicide
The UFO Challenge
The United Nations
The U.S. Congress
The U.S. Presidency
Vanishing Wetlands
Vietnam
Women's Rights
World Hunger
Zoos

# Hazardous Waste

by Keith McGowan

Lucent
Books

LUCENT Overview Series

*To Stacie Heintze, for her friendship and encouragement*

*Acknowledgments are due Kelly Joyce, Melinda Allman, Asia Cutts, Morgan Cutts, Shaun Cutts, Maria Echaniz, Judy Fittery, Pam Greenberg, Dudley D. Greenberg, Jim Hanley of the US EPA Region 8, Stacie Heintze, Chauncy Joyce, Ursula Lennox of the US EPA Region 6, the librarians at the Somerville, Newton, and Cambridge public libraries, Stuart Miller, Lori Shein, and Matt Wilson.*

**Library of Congress Cataloging-in-Publication Data**

McGowan, Keith, 1968–
  Hazardous waste/ by Keith McGowan.
      p.  cm.—(Lucent overview series)
Includes bibliographical references and index.
Summary: Discusses hazardous waste including its disposal and the law, cleaning it up, radioactive waste, hazardous waste and illness, and its incineration, recycling, and reduction.
  ISBN 1-56006-699-7 (hard : alk. paper)
  1. Hazardous wastes—Juvenile literature. [1. Hazardous wastes.
  2. Pollution.] I. Title.  II. Series.
  TD1030.5 .M43 2001
  363.72'87—dc21

                                                            00-009233

# Contents

# Introduction

HAZARDOUS WASTE DISPOSAL is a problem confronting the people of the United States right now. Across the country, Americans are fighting to get hazardous waste cleaned up so that they do not have to live in communities full of toxic contaminants which make them sick. In the northern part of New Orleans, Louisiana, for example, people are living over a buried dump full of toxic chemicals. Approximately 150 contaminants have been found in the soil around their homes, including the heavy metal lead, which can cause physical and mental developmental problems in children, and kidney and nervous system damage in adults. On a June 1999 broadcast of public television's *Lehrer News Hour*, one resident from this neighborhood, Nathan Parker, explained the situation he and his neighbors face: "We are living on a poisoned, toxic site . . . Our kids back there are sick, and we—it's a slow death for us really. We just need to be off of this place." Another resident, Peggy Grandpre, stated, "We have homes that are worthless. You know, we have homes that we can't even rent. No one should be in that situation."[1]

Grandpre, Parker, and others living in this neighborhood have struggled to get the government to buy their homes so they can relocate, move on with their lives, and hopefully recover their health. They have appealed to a government program called Superfund, which was specifically set up to handle emergencies such as theirs, and traveled to Washington, D.C., to promote their struggle. However, the government has been less than responsive. Although the Environmental Protection Agency (EPA) has agreed to clean up their neighborhood, the agency decided simply to dig up two feet of the contaminated soil, lay down a layer of synthetic matting, and place two feet of uncontaminated soil over the mat. Many residents are outraged by this plan. They have received no guarantee that their homes will ever regain their initial value. Nor do they believe that their lives will be free from future exposure to the contaminated soil and garbage. Residents want to move off the site entirely and

*Residents who live near hazardous waste sites like this one often feel that cleanup efforts are inadequate.*

they are stunned that their health and well-being is worth so little that nobody in a position to help them will do anything to get them off of the contaminated site.

Grandpre, Parker, and their neighbors are just a few of the many ordinary people who face this type of situation in the United States. As Brown University sociologist Phil Brown and Harvard Medical School professor Edwin J. Mikkelsen point out in their book *No Safe Place*, hazardous waste contamination is "disturbingly prevalent in this country . . . and it demands immediate attention and drastic remedies."[2]

# 1

# The Hazardous Waste Problem

JUDY FITTERY IS one of the millions of Americans whose life has been affected by the improper disposal of hazardous industrial waste. One hundred yards from her home in Tewksbury, Massachusetts, sits a tract of land once used as a town garbage dump, or landfill. For years, local industries brought their chemical wastes to this landfill and poured them into the ground. The wastes were absorbed by the earth, and have since moved the hundred yards from the landfill border into the soil beneath Fittery's home—helped in their movement by the water of rainstorms and by water flowing underground, which has drawn the chemicals through the earth.

Today, more than fifty hazardous chemical contaminants have been found in Fittery's yard. These contaminants include, among others, the cancer-causing metal arsenic, and the toxic chemical toluene, which is known to cause memory loss, weakness, confusion, nausea, and hearing loss if people are exposed to it for long periods of time. At least some of the fifty contaminants in Fittery's soil are so strong that the underground pipes of her outdoor family pool were eaten away from the outside in, and Fittery was forced to stop planting vegetables in her backyard, because, as an April 1999 State House News Service article explained, "the produce was deformed."[3] Besides the contaminants on Fittery's property, chemical fumes from the landfill sometimes drift into her home on the wind, bringing with them a smell similar to kerosene.

Over the years, Fittery and her family have suffered from a series of life-threatening illnesses which they blame on exposure to this contamination. One member of Fittery's family has already died of Hodgkin's disease—a cancer of the lymph nodes—and another has died of lung cancer. Fittery herself was in and out of the hospital throughout 1999 and 2000; she has had four surgeries for cancer, including a double mastectomy. Her mother, who started experiencing breathing problems when she moved into the house, has since undergone lung surgery and a hysterectomy.

Displaying extraordinary will in the face of these circumstances, Fittery, working together with other local residents, has spent nine years protesting that something be done about the contamination. Town officials, however, have not acted quickly to clean up the landfill, in part, Fittery maintains, because the town itself is responsible for some of the contamination and will have to pay a significant amount toward cleanup.

The state government has also delayed cleanup. The landfill in Fittery's town of Tewksbury is just one of hundreds of severely contaminated sites across Massachusetts, and the state government's Department of Environmental Protection (DEP) has made little or no progress on the cleanup of at least 121 of the 269 most contaminated sites in the state. Under Massachusetts governors William Weld and Paul Cellucci, moreover, funds for the DEP's Bureau of Waste Site Cleanup have been cut from $9.7 million in 1995 to $6.8 million in 1999, slowing the pace of state-sponsored cleanups even further.

In the face of these obstacles, Fittery and other local residents have nevertheless continued to push for action, and it appears that they may have finally been rewarded for their persistence. In 1999, the EPA agreed to consider adding the contaminated landfill to its list of federal National Priority hazardous waste sites, which would open the door for federal money and aid to help clean up the site. The EPA expects to make a decision on the matter in the summer or fall of 2000, and it seems likely that the Tewksbury site will make the list. Possibly, sometime in the next few years, cleanup in Tewksbury will finally begin—more than a decade after Fittery began her protests.

At a 1999 Earth Day press conference, Fittery told reporters what the experience of living for years with hazardous waste contamination had taught her. "Until it's in your own backyard, and at your own back door, you can't understand it," she explained. "If it's not knocking on your door, it's 'Oh, those poor people.' But eventually all those poor people are going to become 'Oh, poor me.' Unless we get this cleaned up, it's going to affect all of us right in our own backyards."[4]

## Contaminated sites in the United States

As Judy Fittery pointed out to reporters on Earth Day 1999, not everyone has hazardous waste contaminating

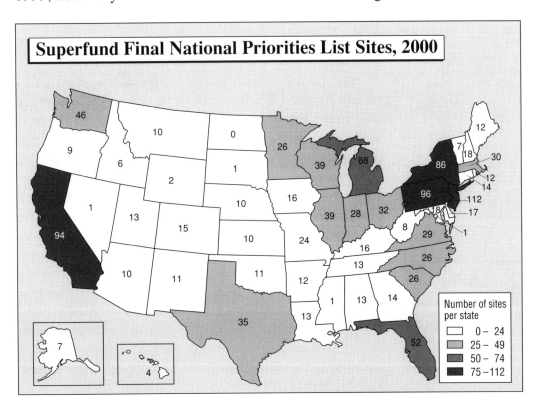

their yards, and not everyone can understand what the experience is like. Nevertheless, the contamination of people's homes with hazardous waste is far from a rare occurrence, and thousands upon thousands of people across the United States face circumstances similar to those of Fittery, her family, and her neighbors. The government's Office of Technology Assessment has estimated that there could be as many as 439,000 contaminated waste sites in the United States. The U.S. General Accounting Office similarly set the maximum figure at 425,000 contaminated sites. Approximately 300,000 of these sites involve old underground gasoline storage tanks—tens of thousands of which are already leaking their hazardous contaminants into the ground. Besides these leaking gas tanks, the remaining 125,000 contaminated sites are the result of industrial, military, and government contamination. At a conservative estimate, more than 19,000 of these sites have been identified by state and territory governments as severely contaminated hazardous waste sites in need of emergency cleanup—similar to the one near Judy Fittery's home— and more than 1,000 sites have been labeled emergency federal National Priority sites by the EPA. In short, every state in the nation has sites contaminated with hazardous waste, and, in most cases, ordinary people are living beside the contamination.

Hazardous waste from these sites has not only contaminated soil. It has also contaminated water supplies. Emergency water supplies have been distributed to more than 350,000 people in the United States because their tap water was discovered to contain dangerously high levels of hazardous contaminants. Wells everywhere across the country have been shut down due to hazardous waste contamination.

Not every person, therefore, has hazardous waste contaminating his or her backyard or tap water. However, there are thousands upon thousands of people in the United States today who do.

## What is hazardous waste?

What is hazardous waste? Hazardous waste is commonly defined as any waste, or garbage, which threatens human health or the environment if it is carelessly thrown away, dumped into the ground, or handled improperly. There are thousands of different chemicals, chemical compounds, and materials that qualify as hazardous waste under this definition. One important category of hazardous waste is "toxic" waste, which can cause illness in people who are exposed to the waste through contaminated tap water, soil, or food. The hazardous wastes toluene and arsenic found in the soil of Judy Fittery's home, for example, are toxic hazardous wastes, since exposure to these chemicals causes a variety of short- and long-term health problems. Toxic wastes are not the only type of hazardous waste, however. Wastes that can easily catch fire, called "ignitable" wastes; wastes that can explode, called "reactive" wastes; and chemical wastes that eat away at the things they touch, called "corrosive" wastes, are all generally considered to be hazardous wastes.

*A container of ignitable, or flammable, waste, one type of hazardous waste.*

Today, industrial plants operating in every state in the nation generate enormous amounts of hazardous waste—altogether millions of tons a year. Facilities generating this waste include electrical utility companies, chemical companies, steel mills, rubber manufacturers, lumber companies, paper mills, plastic manufacturers, oil refineries, mines, defense contractors, textile manufacturers, manufacturers of photographic and medical goods, glass companies, and machinery manufacturers, among others. According to a 1994 paper sponsored by the World Bank, "the United States, as the world's largest producer and consumer of industrial materials, is also probably the world's top producer of toxic [hazardous] wastes."[5]

## Industrial solvents

Industrial chemicals called "solvents" are one of the most common types of hazardous waste generated in the United States today. Solvents are powerful chemical cleansers used by industries to clean and degrease machinery and mechanical parts. Solvents are used by a wide variety of industries, since companies routinely clean machinery as part of their operations, regardless of the type of business they conduct. Manufacturers of electronic equipment, for example, use solvents to clean circuit boards and machinery used during the manufacturing process, while the U.S. Air Force uses solvents to clean and degrease aircraft engines and parts.

One widely used industrial solvent is the chemical trichloroethylene, commonly called "TCE." TCE has been used by industries as a cleansing solvent for decades. Unfortunately, industries have often disposed of spent TCE by simply pouring it into unlined ditches, and this disposal practice has led to the extensive contamination of water supplies in the United States.

For example, at and around the international airport in Tucson, Arizona, defense contractors and other companies—including the Hughes Missile Systems Company, McDonnell Douglas Corporation, and General Dynamics Corporation—used TCE to degrease airplane parts and engines, and then disposed of the spent TCE by pouring the chemical waste into the ground. The TCE dumped by these companies seeped through the earth and contaminated groundwater supplies that served as a source of tap water for as many as 47,000 people. Wells in the area were ultimately shut down, but not before some people in Tucson unknowingly drank TCE-contaminated water for as many as ten or twenty years. People who drink water contaminated with TCE for long periods of time may suffer from liver and kidney damage, damage to the immune system—the system in the body which protects people from illness—and, in the case of pregnant women, harm to the development of the fetus. Drinking TCE-contaminated water has also been linked to the onset of childhood leukemia, a disease which is often fatal.

The contamination of tap water in Tucson is only one of many instances of TCE contamination across the country. Wells in Albuquerque, New Mexico; Atwater, California; Arden Hills, Minnesota; Spokane, Washington; and Parker Ford, Pennsylvania—to name a few—have all been closed due to high levels of TCE contamination. According to a fact sheet released by the EPA, studies show that between 9 and 34 percent of the nation's water may be contaminated with TCE, although much of this contamination is at levels currently believed to be safe to drink. More than 40 percent of the most contaminated hazardous waste sites in the United States contain TCE as one of the contaminants.

## Perchloroethylene (perc) and dry cleaners

Besides TCE, industries use a number of other industrial solvents that are afterward disposed of as hazardous wastes, including one called perchloroethylene, or perc for short. Like TCE, perc is used by industries to clean and degrease machinery and mechanical parts. Unlike TCE, however, perc is also the main chemical used by dry cleaning stores. Although many people are unaware of the practice, dry cleaners traditionally clean clothes by soaking them in a bath of the solvent perc.

Because dry cleaning stores are so common in the United States, the disposal of perc has become a major

*Dry cleaners usually clean clothes with perc, an industrial solvent that can contaminate the local water supply if disposed of improperly.*

environmental problem. Although a single dry cleaner generates much less hazardous waste than a large industrial plant, even one such business can dispose of enough perc to have a real impact on the environment and public health. In many towns, small dry cleaning operations have disposed of perc simply by draining it into the ground, and in some cases this perc has sunk into the earth and contaminated underground drinking water supplies. Drinking perc-contaminated water for long periods of time may cause liver damage and other serious health problems.

The wealthy suburb of Great Neck, New York, is just one of many towns to have had its water supply contaminated by a dry cleaner. This perc-contaminated site in Great Neck is now listed by the EPA as one of the most contaminated sites in the country.

## Heavy metals

Industrial solvents such as TCE and perc are one class of hazardous wastes that pose a considerable threat to public health in the United States. Another common group of hazardous wastes that pose a serious public health threat are called "heavy metals." Heavy metals include lead, mercury, chromium, cadmium, arsenic, copper, and nickel, among others. Although many may not think of metals as hazardous substances, long-term exposure to heavy metals—through the regular consumption of contaminated tap water or the routine inhalation of small motes of metal dust—can cause an array of serious illnesses. Exposure to even small amounts of lead, for example, can cause kidney damage, high blood pressure, anemia—associated with low levels of oxygen in the bloodstream—problems with memory, and damage to the nerves and brain. Children exposed to lead may suffer damage to their mental and physical development and thus suffer from learning disabilities, low attention spans, and problems with coordination.

Lead is only one heavy metal that can cause illness. Exposure to the heavy metal chromium can cause skin ulcers, breathing problems, and cancer, among other health problems. Exposure to the heavy metal arsenic is similarly associated with a range of cancers, including cancer of the skin, bone marrow, lymph glands, and lungs, according to the federal Occupational Safety and Health Administration (OSHA).

Just as industrial solvents such as TCE and perc are used by a wide range of industries involved in many different types of manufacturing processes, so too are heavy metals commonly used by many industries involved in the manufacture of a wide range of products. Heavy metals such as lead and cadmium, for example, are used in the manufacture of paint to give the color of the paint a hard, bright quality. Heavy metals are also used in the manufacture of plastics to make the plastics less transparent and more durable. Heavy metals play a significant role in the manufacture of batteries, circuit boards, and other electronic products. Even the chemical industry uses heavy metals as part of its chemical manufacturing process, since metals have unique chemical properties that the chemical industry has been able to exploit. All of these industries end up with heavy metals as waste, which must be disposed of with extreme caution so as not to contaminate water supplies or soil.

As is the case with industrial solvents, however, heavy metals have all too often been disposed of recklessly, contaminating soil and water at thousands of sites across the United States. Mining companies, for example, have often left vast swaths of land piled high with sandy deposits of heavy metals called "tailings," tiny rocks containing small amounts of unmined metals. Traditionally, these companies have abandoned this sandy waste in neglected piles left to blow away on the wind, drift into local creeks, and otherwise spread into the environment.

Hundreds of square miles in Deer Lodge Valley, Montana, for example, were contaminated with lead, cadmium, zinc, arsenic, and copper, primarily due to the past operations of the Anaconda Minerals Company ore-processing facility. Meanwhile, in Alpine County, California, heavy metals were left in holding ponds by the operators of the now defunct Leviathan Mine. During the early spring months of 1998 and 1999 these heavy metals overflowed into nearby creeks feeding into the Carson River, a main source of tap water for people living near the river in Douglas County, Nevada. Talking to *Las Vegas Review-Journal* reporter Sandra Chereb, Senator Richard Bryan of Nevada recently expressed concern over the situation at Leviathan Mine. Bryan stated that the heavy metal contamination of the nearby creeks "could result in an environmental disaster if not effectively cleaned up."[6]

Mining companies have left their mark on the American landscape by abandoning heavy metals throughout the West. However, they are not the only businesses to have disposed of heavy metals irresponsibly. A tannery in the Appalachian hills of Middlesboro, Kentucky, for example, routinely released the heavy metal chromium along with other hazardous wastes into a local waterway called Yellow Creek. At the time, Yellow Creek was used as a source of

*A worker crosses a pile of tailings, mining waste that can contaminate the environment with heavy metals.*

tap water by people living downstream, and many of these people fell ill. One resident recalled: "Every family told of kidney troubles, vomiting, diarrhea, rashes. One family showed us big welts right after they showered. And there were huge numbers of miscarriages. I cried every night."[7] Residents organized into a neighborhood association and struggled hard to stop this release of hazardous waste into the creek. Ultimately, they were successful in their struggle. The tannery stopped its releases and, after six years, Yellow Creek was cleaned up. The contamination of Yellow Creek is just one example of the incredible harm which heavy metals can cause when disposed of improperly.

## Polychlorinated biphenyls (PCBs)

Industrial solvents and heavy metals are two types of common hazardous wastes. A class of oily, human-made chemicals called polychlorinated biphenyls, or "PCBs," are another type of hazardous waste that has caused significant environmental damage in the United States and threatened the health of millions of people over the years.

PCBs were once considered ideal liquids for use inside of electrical equipment because they could withstand high temperatures without catching fire, and they were first used for this purpose in 1929, when the Monsanto Chemical Company began manufacturing PCBs commercially. Over the years, many other uses for PCBs were also found. As writer Jim Detjen explains in the book *Who's Poisoning America?:* "The many products that have contained PCBs at one time or another are ironing-board covers, highway striping paints, bread wrappers, toilet soaps, safety glass . . . upholstering materials, cereal boxes . . . varnishes, [and] lacquers."[8]

At first, few people concerned themselves with the potential environmental and health hazards of PCBs. In the late 1960s, however, the toxic effects of PCBs became clear in part due to two tragic accidents in Asia—one in Japan in 1968 and the other in Taiwan in 1969. In both instances, rice oil was contaminated with PCBs and thousands of people were poisoned after eating food cooked in this contaminated oil. Victims of the poisoning suffered from pustules on the skin, headaches, nausea, diarrhea, fever, and the liver disease hepatitis.

Despite increasing signs of the dangers of PCB exposure in the 1970s, however, the production of PCBs in the United States peaked in the early 1970s at approximately 80 to 85 million pounds per year. This widespread production and use of PCBs led to significant environmental contamination. The Hudson River in New York, for example, was contaminated by two General Electric plants that manufactured electrical capacitors in upstate New York. Each of these plants routinely released as much as twenty-five to thirty pounds of PCB waste a day into the Hudson. Similarly, the Great Lakes became contaminated from the release of PCBs as waste into the lakes by industrial plants along the shoreline. Fish in the Hudson River and the Great Lakes absorbed so much of these PCBs that a warning against eating large bass from the Hudson River was issued in August 1975, and warnings against eating fish from the Great Lakes were also announced during the same time period. Recognizing the growing threat to public health posed by the unchecked use of PCBs in the United States, Congress took a rare step and outlawed the manufacture and distribution of PCBs—in most cases—as part of a broader environmental law called the Toxic Substance Control Act (TSCA) of 1976.

Despite this congressional action, however, PCBs are still commonly found today in the waste that industries throw away every year, in large part because some older machinery now in operation was manufactured when PCBs were still in widespread use, and, when industrial plants dispose of the aging equipment, they also dispose of the PCBs inside. In 1995, for example, General Electric disposed of

*Decontaminated soil pours from the conveyor belt of a thermal treatment system at a Superfund site contaminated with PCBs.*

more than forty-six tons of out-of-service transformers, transformer oil, ballasts, and other PCB-contaminated debris from its plant in Selkirk, New York.

Because PCBs do not break down easily in the environment, the PCB contamination of the Great Lakes and the Hudson River continues to this day, and fish advisories are still in effect, warning people not to eat too many fish from these waters. Research finished in 1998 by the government's National Institute of Environmental Health Services (NIEHS) concluded that "PCB contamination of the

*Paper mills like this one often produce dioxins as a by-product of bleaching paper with chlorine. Exposure to dioxins can cause many diseases, including cancer.*

Hudson River will persist for decades and that consumption of fish from the river will, therefore, pose continuing hazards to human health."[9] PCBs can be found in more than one in five of the most contaminated hazardous waste sites in the United States.

## Dioxins and paper mills

Dioxins, a class of chemicals related to PCBs, are another group of toxic chemicals that greatly concern environmentalists and government officials. Like PCBs, dioxins do not break down easily in the environment, so dioxins released by industries today are expected to last for decades to come.

Dioxins are different from industrial solvents, heavy metals, and many other hazardous wastes because they are not purposely used by industries. Rather, dioxins are created as useless by-products during certain chemical processes involving the chemical chlorine. Paper mills, for example, are a major source of dioxins, since paper mills often use chlorine when they bleach paper, and dioxins are created during this process.

Once created, dioxins need to be disposed of with extreme caution, since exposure to even small amounts can cause a range of serious health problems, including cancer, skin disease, and liver damage. However, dioxins have not always been disposed of with care. In particular, paper mills, which are traditionally built on the banks of rivers, have often released dioxins into these rivers. Paper mills in Maine, for example, have so contaminated the Penobscot, Androscoggin, and Kennebec Rivers that fish living in those rivers have absorbed high levels of dioxin into their bodies. The State of Maine Department of Health Services today warns people against eating fish from these rivers. In particular, the Maine Department of Health Services advises that people never eat fish caught in the Kennebec River, eat no more than six to twelve meals a year of fish caught in the Androscoggin River, and eat no more than twelve to twenty-four meals a year of fish caught in the Penobscot River.

Dioxins are not only contained in river fish. Dioxins can also be found in beef, poultry, and dairy products, and most Americans receive their highest doses of dioxins when they eat these foods. The federal government is so concerned with widespread dioxin contamination that President Bill Clinton announced a new initiative in October 1999, requiring companies that release as little as a tenth of a gram of dioxin as waste to report this amount to the government, starting on January 1, 2000.

## The generation of hazardous waste today

Although hazardous waste is recognized today as a serious environmental and public health problem, statistics suggest that the production of hazardous waste is actually on the rise. In 1997, large commercial manufacturers in the United States generated approximately 40.7 million tons of hazardous waste, an increase of 4.4 million tons, or 11 percent, since 1995. During those same years, again considering only large commercial manufacturers, the amount of wastewater contaminated with toxic hazardous waste released into the nation's rivers, lakes, and streams also increased, from 176 million pounds in 1995 to 218 million pounds in 1997—an increase of 24 percent, or about one-quarter. Environmentalists are concerned that the present increase in hazardous waste generation will worsen the nation's problems with environmental contamination.

# 2

# The Disposal of Hazardous Wastes and the Law

THE DISPOSAL OF hazardous waste is a problem that people have been struggling with for more than half a century. As early as 1944, scientists understood that the disposal of industrial wastes threatened the American environment and public health. In that year, an article entitled "The Industrial Waste Problem" described how the improper disposal of industrial wastes could badly contaminate American lakes, rivers, and underground water. "Certain wastes must be particularly treated to prevent poisoning of surface and underground water supplies," the article explained. "Some types of wastes discharged into . . . underground water supplies result in far-reaching damage."[10]

Ten years later, in 1954, researcher W. C. Webb echoed this warning, expressing special concern over the dumping of hazardous industrial wastes in local landfills meant for household garbage. Speaking at an industrial waste conference that brought together people from industry, universities, and the government to discuss the issue, Webb cautioned: "A sanitary landfill must not be used if there is any possibility of polluting either surface or groundwater supplies." In particular, Webb pointed out that "soluble chemicals" would "add their properties to leaching water," which meant that rainwater would draw industrial chemicals through the soil with it, threatening to contaminate underground water supplies. "The industry contemplating a sanitary landfill would do well to check . . . as to the possibilities of water contamination,"[11] Webb concluded.

During those same decades, however, industries routinely dumped their hazardous chemical wastes into ditches, spread the wastes across fields, or poured the wastes into rivers and lakes, ignoring the warnings of scientists and engineers of the time. Looking back at those years in their book *The Law of Hazardous Wastes and Toxic Substances*, environmental lawyers John Sprankling and Gregory Weber explain bluntly: "American factories, refineries, mines, and other business enterprises disposed of hazardous wastes in the cheapest possible manner, with little or no concern for human health or the environment."[12]

The reckless dumping of hazardous industrial wastes went unchecked for decades. Even disposal sites designed to take industrial wastes did little to protect public health or the surrounding land and waterways. At one such industrial waste disposal site in Kansas City, Missouri, for example, operators accepted waste for more than fifteen years—through the 1960s and into the 1970s—collecting more than fifty million gallons of industrial waste from companies such as AT&T Technologies, the FMC Corporation,

and the International Business Machines Corporation. Operators dug six basins—five of them holes in the ground and the sixth with walls—and poured much of the waste into these basins. As a result, thousands of contaminants sank into groundwater supplies and were carried into the nearby Missouri and Blue Rivers. Soil on the site, meanwhile, became contaminated with countless wastes, including the heavy metals cadmium and chromium, and the toxic chemicals benzene, toluene, and vinyl chloride—all of which cause short- and long-term illnesses if people are exposed to them. This special disposal facility became yet another site which would ultimately need to be cleaned up to protect the health of people living nearby.

## The Resource Conservation and Recovery Act (RCRA)

In the late 1960s, the American public grew more environmentally conscious, and hazardous waste contamination became an important issue. Responding to growing public pressure, the federal government finally turned to confront the issue. In 1976, Congress passed the first federal law focused on the disposal of solid hazardous wastes, the Resource Conservation and Recovery Act (RCRA, pronounced "rick-ra").

RCRA set basic rules for the handling, storage, and disposal of hazardous wastes. Under RCRA, industries were required to keep track of the amount of hazardous wastes they generated and report this amount to the government. If hazardous wastes were sent offsite for disposal, only approved transportation companies could be used to transport the wastes, and only specially licensed "treatment, storage, and disposal" (TSD) facilities could accept the wastes. If hazardous wastes were kept onsite, which was and still is often the case, the industrial plant itself became a type of hazardous waste treatment, storage, and disposal facility under RCRA, subject to licensing and special requirements. No matter what was done with the wastes, RCRA required that paperwork be filled out along the way, allowing the government to track hazardous waste from its creation to its disposal, or, as is sometimes said, "from cradle to grave."

RCRA helped ease the nation's problems with hazardous waste contamination. The law restrained the previously unrestricted dumping of hazardous wastes, promoting the cautious handling of waste instead. RCRA requirements added significantly to the cost of hazardous waste disposal, creating an incentive for companies to generate less waste and therefore save money. RCRA also gave the government a view into the hazardous waste problem by allowing the government to track the types and quantities of waste being generated by industries in the United States. Previous to that time, the federal government had no record of hazardous waste creation, movement, and disposal.

However, RCRA did not solve the problem of hazardous waste disposal. In fact, RCRA sanctioned the creation and disposal of hazardous waste by allowing companies to do so legally, as long as they followed basic guidelines. Under RCRA, hazardous waste was still being dumped into the ground, held in unlined storage pools, or otherwise released into the environment.

## The Land Ban

Recognizing early on that the rules set forth by RCRA did not resolve the hazardous waste problem, Congress strengthened RCRA through a series of amendments passed in 1984. In particular, Congress enacted a rule called the Land Ban, which prohibited the disposal of hazardous waste on land unless the waste was "treated" first. The Land Ban went into full effect on May 8, 1990. As of today, the Land Ban has been the law for more than a decade.

In theory, the Land Ban should have gone a long way toward addressing the issue of hazardous waste dumping. Certainly, the title of the amendment suggested a strong stance against the disposal of hazardous waste, one beyond that of simple regulation. In practice, however, the Land Ban has not lived up to its promise, in large part because the ban set its definition of "treated" hazardous wastes very broadly. The treated hazardous wastes which the Land Ban allows to be disposed of on land are often still hazardous.

Under the Land Ban, for example, treating hazardous waste sometimes requires no more than simply mixing the waste with cement or some other hardening agent. When placed into the ground, waste treated in this way will take much longer to move into the surrounding soil. However, the hazardous waste is not destroyed by this treatment; its spread is simply slowed.

Alternately, treatment can mean separating hazardous waste out from a larger mix of nonhazardous liquids, so that the volume of hazardous waste is less in the end. This separation can be accomplished through a variety of processes, including a chemical process called "precipitation," which causes the waste to form as a solid out of the liquid mix; a physical process called "centrifugation," where the waste is spun so fast that the heavier components move toward the outside of the mix; or through the simple use of filters. These processes separate hazardous wastes out from a larger mix of waste and concentrate the hazardous wastes into a purer form, so that industries ultimately dispose of a smaller quantity of contaminated waste. However, this type of treatment does not eliminate or neutralize the hazardous wastes; it simply reduces the volume of waste. Thus, this type of treated waste is still hazardous, and it still poses the threat of contamination when placed into the ground.

The Land Ban has forced companies to treat hazardous wastes in some way before they dispose of these wastes on land, and thus has slowed the movement of wastes into the environment. However, even with the Land Ban in effect, vast amounts of hazardous waste are still placed into the ground each year in forms that can spread into surrounding land and groundwater, causing contamination.

## The double liner design for landfills

Besides the Land Ban, the RCRA amendments of 1984 also included an important provision dictating the design of hazardous waste landfills. Because of this provision, hazardous waste landfills today need to have a double liner along their bottom and sides. These liners are typically made of synthetic materials or clay and they help hold the hazardous waste in place. A pump must be placed between the two liners so that when the first liner cracks and hazardous waste begins to leak out, the waste can be pumped back into the landfill before it breaches the second liner. Monitoring

*Radioactive and chemical waste is dumped at a disposal facility where it will be stored in a clay-lined pit.*

wells are also generally required around the landfill. These wells are periodically checked to see if hazardous waste is leaking into the groundwater beneath the landfill and escaping away from the site. Finally, once the landfill is full of waste, it must be capped so that the wastes cannot easily evaporate into the air or blow away on the wind.

The two-liner design for modern landfills is far superior to the hole-in-the-ground landfill design of previous decades. Nevertheless, just as the Land Ban did not resolve the problem of hazardous waste disposal, so too regulations for the design of landfills are not a permanent solution to the problem either. Rather, the new landfill design is once again simply a mechanism for postponing the spread of hazardous waste. Liners may hold waste in place for decades, but eventually even the best liners will crack and leak. In her book *Salvaging the Land of Plenty*, environmentalist and government foreign policymaker Jennifer Seymour Whitaker explains: "As long as dumps are part of the waste equation, the threats to groundwater and air cannot be effectively alleviated by state-of-the-art liners, pumps, pipes, or vents alone." All landfill liners, Whitaker notes, "will eventually deteriorate."[13] Decades from now, the young people of today and future generations of Americans will likely face the problem of old, leaking landfills—landfills designed to last longer but not forever.

RCRA and the RCRA amendments have undeniably had a real impact on the disposal of hazardous waste. There can be no comparison between past unrestricted hazardous waste disposal practices and the regulated disposal of hazardous wastes today. Hazardous wastes must now be treated before they are disposed of on land, and they are typically then placed in landfills with double liners—or sometimes even in closed tanks—that can safely retain hazardous wastes for decades. Nevertheless, the government has not been able to fundamentally solve the hazardous waste disposal problem using these laws. Hazardous wastes are still disposed of on land and they are still expected to spread into the environment over time, contaminating water supplies and soil, and threatening the health of people living nearby.

## The Clean Water Act

Hazardous waste is not only disposed of on land. Companies also dispose of hazardous wastes by releasing the wastes into rivers, lakes, and other bodies of water. Primarily, these releases are governed by the Clean Water Act, which was passed by Congress in 1972. The Clean Water Act sets limits on the amount of contaminated wastewater which industrial plants can release into waterways. To set this limit, the EPA—which is charged with enforcing the act—typically looks for the company using the best technology currently available for reducing contaminants in wastewater, and then requires that other companies either use this technology or match its level of contaminant reduction. This method for setting standards is called the "best available technology" model. Under the Clean Water Act, moreover, if the contamination in a given river, lake, or waterway poses a serious threat to public health even with the use of the best available technology, the EPA can set stricter limits requiring that companies further reduce their releases.

The Clean Water Act has greatly reduced the amount of waste released into the nation's surface waters. However, just as RCRA allows for the legal disposal of hazardous waste on land, so too the Clean Water Act allows industrial plants everywhere to release wastes into the nation's waterways legally, in a manner sanctioned by the government. The Clean Water Act has therefore not stopped the release of hazardous wastes into surface waters. In fact, under the act, hundreds of millions of pounds of wastewater contaminated with toxic waste are legally poured into the nation's rivers, lakes, and waterways each year.

## Industrial wastes excused from hazardous waste laws

One of the greatest controversies currently surrounding the disposal of hazardous wastes centers around the fact that some hazardous wastes have been exempted from federal hazardous waste regulations altogether, through a law called the Bevill Amendment. The Bevill Amendment exempts certain wastes

*Industrial waste pours into a waterway. The Clean Water Act allows for the release of some types of industrial waste into our nation's rivers, lakes, and streams.*

from hazardous waste laws even when these wastes are toxic to humans and even when their disposal causes environmental harm. Certain wastes created when companies drill for and refine oil, for example, have been exempted from federal hazardous waste laws even though they contain toxic chemicals and would normally qualify as hazardous wastes.

The EPA has offered a variety of reasons for exempting these oil wastes from hazardous waste regulations. The EPA has claimed that hazardous waste regulations do not "provide sufficient flexibility to consider costs and avoid the serious economic impacts that regulation would create for the [oil] industry's exploration and production operations." The EPA has further insisted that "existing State and Federal regulatory programs are generally adequate for controlling oil," and that "permitting delays would hinder new facilities, disrupting the search for new oil and gas deposits."[14] Environmental Defense, however, a mainstream environmental group based in New York City, is one of many environmental groups to offer a different explanation for the oil waste exemptions. Some hazardous oil wastes have been exempted from hazardous waste laws, Environmental Defense maintains, because of the power of the oil industry. The group explains: "Powerful lobbies, such as the petroleum industry, have managed to keep their wastes from being legally designated 'hazardous.'"[15]

Since some wastes are exempt from federal hazardous waste laws, companies have been allowed to dispose of them with less than the usual care given for public health and environmental concerns. For example, millions of gallons of oil waste containing benzene, lead, barium, and other contaminants have been placed in open pits just yards from the town of Grand Bois, Louisiana. Residents of Grand Bois regularly complain of burning eyes, breathing problems, and headaches, and they maintain that it is the fumes from these oil-waste pits that are poisoning them. Despite their complaints, however, oil companies continue to dispose of the wastes in these pits. The Louisiana state government could pass its own, special restrictions on the waste; but, as of May 1999 the Louisiana government had decided against stricter regulation. "Oil and gas is the heart and soul of Louisiana," insisted state senator Craig Romero. "Oil and gas provides a lot of jobs in Louisiana. It's not important enough to forget about our people's well-being, but don't let people sensationalize and scare you into something that's not really there."[16]

Scientists from Louisiana State University have called for the closing of the Grand Bois oil-waste pits, pointing out that some people living in Grand Bois have already been shown to have high levels of barium and lead in their bodies. Many residents in Grand Bois are deeply disturbed that the oil wastes have been allowed to slip through the cracks of hazardous waste legislation. One resident expressed a representative view: "It's scary to know that our government would allow this to go on."[17]

Environmental groups are currently fighting to close the loopholes left open by the Bevill Amendment. Thanks to a suit brought against the EPA by Environmental Defense, the EPA announced in August 1998 that four types of oil wastes previously excused from hazardous waste regulation would be listed as hazardous. However, the EPA decided against listing ten other oil wastes as hazardous wastes, and these wastes continue to be exempted from federal hazardous waste regulations. Besides certain oil wastes, some hazardous wastes generated by mining operations have also been exempted from hazardous waste regulation under the Bevill Amendment.

## Environmental justice

The exemption of some wastes from hazardous waste laws has proven to be controversial. Another controversy surrounding the disposal of hazardous waste centers on the role which income level and ethnicity play in disposal decisions. Since the early 1980s, environmentalists and civil rights activists have raised concerns that minority communities and

*Members of community and environmental groups protest a medical waste incinerator which pollutes their neighborhood.*

*These barrels of toxic waste were illegally dumped on Native American territory.*

communities of people earning modest, working-class incomes were being singled out to bear the burden of the hazardous waste disposal problem.

In 1982, this issue became the focal point of protests in North Carolina. At the time, the North Carolina government needed a place to dispose of soil contaminated with 30,000 gallons of PCBs, and the state government selected Warren County in North Carolina as the disposal site. The people living in Warren County had the lowest average income in the state, and 65 percent of the population was African American. Residents in Warren County protested vigorously that their community had been unfairly chosen for the PCB landfill because they were a low-income, minority community. As environmental professor Ken Geiser and immunology student Gerry Waneck would later point out, the site was not scientifically the most suitable, since groundwater used by nearby residents passed only five to ten feet below the surface of the proposed dumping grounds. The Southern Christian Leadership Conference and the Congressional

Black Caucus were two of many groups that helped local residents lead demonstrations against the proposed site. However, residents were jailed when they protested, and the demonstrations were ultimately unsuccessful. The PCBs were placed in Warren County, in the town of Afton, directly over shallow groundwater supplies.

Since that time, several studies have found that people of color and people with low incomes are shouldering more than their fair share of the hazardous waste disposal problem. In 1987, for example, a study conducted by the United Church of Christ (UCC) found a clear relationship between the placement of hazardous waste facilities and the race of the people who lived nearby. In particular, the study found that there was "an inordinate concentration of such sites in Black and Hispanic communities."[18] Hazardous waste facilities were also more likely to be located in low-income neighborhoods, the UCC study found, but even among these low-income neighborhoods, hazardous waste facilities were particularly placed in locations where fewer white Americans lived. A 1990 University of Michigan study reached a similar conclusion when studying Detroit, finding that "a minority resident is about four times more likely than a white citizen to live within a mile of a [hazardous waste] site."[19]

Responding to these studies and to hazardous waste dumping in their communities, grassroots organizations across the country have formed to fight against the unequal distribution of hazardous waste contamination, which concerns not only African Americans, but also Hispanic and Native American people. Together, they have defined a new principle called "environmental justice." Environmental justice means, broadly, that all people have the right to live in a clean environment regardless of race, class, national origin, or other characteristics by which society often discriminates. Grassroots organizations that have taken up the call for environmental justice include the Southwest Organizing Project in Albuquerque, New Mexico, the Gulf Coast Tenants Association in Louisiana, and the People United for a Better Oakland (PUEBLO) in Oakland, California. Mainstream environmental groups have also taken strong stands on this issue. The

Sierra Club, for example, states that "in order to fulfill our mission of environmental protection and a sustainable future for the planet, we must ensure social justice and human rights . . . environmental justice issues need to be addressed to protect the health and safety of citizens, particularly minorities, residing in low income communities."[20]

The work of these grassroots and national environmental groups has not gone unnoticed by the government. Recognizing the numerous studies that have demonstrated how hazardous waste disposal facilities are more often located in minority and working-class communities, President Bill Clinton issued an executive order in 1994 directing the EPA to develop a strategy to address the issue of environmental justice. The EPA has since issued guidelines stating that decisions for the siting of hazardous waste facilities must take into account the race and income of those living nearby. Business groups and state governments have argued against the EPA's policy, insisting that it will be too difficult and costly to implement. Some have pointed out that industrial facilities bring not only waste with them, but also jobs that are much needed in low-income neighborhoods. However, as environmental justice activist Charles Streadit, president of Houston's Northeast Community Action Group, explained in an interview, "We need all the money we can get to upgrade our school system. But we shouldn't have to be poisoned to get improvements for our children."[21]

## "It makes you wonder what you could dig up"

Although minorities and people with modest incomes bear an unfair portion of the hazardous waste problem, this does not mean that hazardous waste contamination is found only in minority and working-class communities. To the contrary, countless middle-class and wealthy communities have been contaminated by hazardous waste. The exclusive suburb of Spring Valley, California, is one example. Spring Valley was built in an area once used by the United States military to test poison gas, and contamination from these tests still remains beneath the houses of this suburb. Resident William Harrop was one of those in town surprised to find that his neighborhood was built over contamination. "When even a quiet place like ours can have a background like this," Harrop admitted to a *Los Angeles Times* reporter, "it makes you wonder what you could dig up just about anywhere."[22]

# 3

# Cleaning Up
# Hazardous Waste

THE EFFORT TO clean up the nation's contaminated hazardous waste sites began in the suburb of Niagara Falls, New York. There, over the course of more than a decade, a company called the Hooker Chemical Corporation buried twenty-two thousand tons of hazardous waste—in barrels and in liquid form—in a partially dug trench called Love Canal. Afterward, an elementary school, playground, and homes were built on top and along the border of the buried waste. The chemical dumping in Niagara Falls took place in the 1940s and early 1950s, and, by the 1970s, few if any of the residents living near the buried chemical waste site knew of its existence. People only discovered the contamination in the late 1970s when, among other things, they noticed an occasional bad smell in the neighborhood, and toxic contamination was found in the basement of a nearby home. Reading about the buried waste in the local newspaper, one homemaker, Lois Gibbs, connected exposure to these chemicals with seizures that her five-year-old son had started experiencing shortly after he began his kindergarten class. Her son's elementary school, she found out, had been built directly on top of the contaminated site. Concerned about the connection between her son's illness and exposure to the wastes, Gibbs went door to door alerting her neighbors to the buried waste and asking whether others had suffered from abnormal illnesses. She quickly learned that people living near the contamination had experienced a range of health problems—including miscarriages, severe migraines, kidney bleeding, intestinal problems, and cancer.

## "I guess you just do what you have to"

By the time she was done talking to people in her neighborhood, Gibbs had started unknowingly on a path of leadership, and would soon be organizing her neighbors into a group demanding that something be done about the contamination. In a November 1999 newspaper interview Gibbs recalled those difficult times: "At first I was really terrified to be the leader for the families at Love Canal. I was kind of shy then and I had never spoken in public before. . . . But when we started to really organize our effort, I just happened to be the one everyone looked to because I had been the one to go door to door asking questions and telling people what was going on in the first place. I guess you just do what you have to when your family and children are at stake."[23]

Organized by Gibbs and her old schoolmate, homemaker Debbie Cerrillo, the people of Niagara Falls quickly ran into

*Lois Gibbs (left) and Debbie Cerrillo led the fight to clean up Love Canal.*

an obstacle—one that, in later years, people fighting against contamination in other communities would often encounter. The local, state, and federal governments refused to take serious steps to clean up the hazardous waste at Love Canal and protect the health of those living in the community. In an effort to spur the government into action, Gibbs, Cerrillo, and other affected residents worked tirelessly with scientist Beverly Paigen from the New York State Department of Health to document the abnormally frequent health problems in their neighborhood. They traveled to the state capitol, Albany, and the nation's capitol, Washington, D.C., lobbying government officials for a resolution to their problem. In particular, they demanded not only a cleanup of the buried hazardous waste, but also money so that those living closest to the contamination could move away; now that their homes were valueless, there was little hope that they could sell the property and obtain money to relocate. In a fit of desperation, the residents of Niagara Falls even held two EPA officials hostage for several hours when the government refused to help pay for the relocation of families.

Ultimately, the people of Niagara Falls were successful in their efforts. Their plight was recognized by the government as an emergency, and funds were freed up to help residents move away from the contamination.

The efforts of the Niagara Falls residents had an impact far beyond the resolution of their own problem. Because the people living near Love Canal were able to get national newspaper and television coverage of their situation, the nation saw firsthand what it was like to live near a contaminated site. The public witnessed the government's inaction

*A pool of toxic waste from Love Canal lies in the yard of an abandoned home.*

and the extreme measures which Niagara Falls residents were forced to take to affect change. In particular, it became increasingly clear to people everywhere across the country that there was no program in place to handle similar emergencies in the future. The efforts of the Niagara Falls residents therefore set in motion a national movement focused on the issue of abandoned hazardous waste sites. People everywhere demanded that the federal government have a program in place to handle similar emergencies.

The end result of this movement was a federal law, the Comprehensive Environmental Response, Compensation, and Liability Act (CERCLA), commonly called the Superfund law—the first national law concerning itself entirely with the cleanup of contaminated hazardous waste sites. It was signed on December 11, 1980, as one of President Jimmy Carter's last acts, two months after Carter had flown to Niagara Falls himself to sign an agreement with New York State supplying $15 million to buy Love Canal residents' homes.

*A warning sign at Love Canal.*

## The Superfund law

The Superfund law created a special government trust fund where money could be set aside to pay for emergencies arising from hazardous waste contamination. Superfund also charged the federal government with identifying and cleaning up the worst hazardous waste sites in the country. Importantly, Superfund was designed so that ordinary taxpayers would not be saddled with the cost of paying for cleanups and emergency actions. Superfund adopted a "polluter pays" principle. The companies responsible for contamination would be required to pay for cleanups whenever possible.

Despite hopes that Superfund would quickly resolve the problem of hazardous waste contamination across the country, its early years were not a success. This was due in part to a series of scandals at the EPA—the government agency charged with overseeing Superfund cleanups—in the first years after Superfund's passage. Under then-president Ronald Reagan, controversial individuals were named to direct the EPA and head up the EPA's toxic waste programs—individuals who did not appear to be committed to protecting the environment. As *New York Times* reporter Philip Shabecoff explains in his book *A Fierce Green Fire*, Congress launched an investigation of these individuals and the EPA in general in the early 1980s, and found, in 1982, "evidence of cronyism with industry, illegal private meetings with representatives of regulated companies, and sweetheart deals in which chemical waste dumpers were allowed to settle with the agency at a fraction of what it would cost to clean up the dangerous mess they had created."[24] Ultimately, both the director of the EPA and the head of the EPA's toxic waste programs were forced to step down, and the head of the EPA's toxic waste programs, in particular, was sentenced to six months in prison for lying to Congress.

Superfund clearly could not accomplish its goals under such management. By 1986, however, several years after the scandals had subsided and with the agency under less controversial leadership, the EPA had still managed to clean up only six sites nationwide. Abandoned hazardous waste sites were far more common than many had realized, and the cleanup of each of these sites proved to be a complex and difficult task. Recognizing these facts, Congress voted that year to strengthen Superfund by raising the trust fund—the money used to pay for emergency actions, and for cleanups when responsible companies could not pay the entire cost—from $1.6 billion to $8.5 billion. This trust fund was primarily financed through taxes on crude oil, certain chemicals, and through a special environmental tax on businesses. Congress also gave the president and EPA broader powers to force companies to pay for cleanups. Both Republicans and Democrats overwhelmingly supported these changes; the vote was a sweeping 88 to 8 in the Senate and 386 to 27 in the House of Representatives. With the image of Love Canal still fresh in the public's mind, politicians were under considerable pressure to show that they were committed to cleaning up hazardous waste sites and protecting public health.

Since that time, the Superfund program has been able to claim some modest successes. On May 12, 1999, EPA head Carol Browner highlighted these successes in testimony before members of the House of Representatives. Browner noted, for example, that more than five thousand emergency removal actions have been taken under Superfund to date, to "immediately reduce the threat to public health and the environment." Browner also pointed out that, using money from Superfund, the EPA had "supplied over 350,000 people with alternative water supplies in order to protect them from contaminated groundwater and surface water."[25] Furthermore, approximately fifteen hundred of the nation's worst hazardous waste sites have been placed on Superfund's National Priority list for cleanup, and, as of October 1998, 585 of these sites had reached the final stages of cleanup.

*EPA head, Carol Browner.*

## Superfund cleanups are sometimes inadequate

Under Superfund, the EPA has overseen the cleanup of sites that may not otherwise have been cleaned up if Superfund did not exist. For this effort, environmentalists applaud the program. Nevertheless, environmentalists and residents living near contamination have sometimes criticized the EPA for performing a less than adequate job on its Superfund cleanups. Some people who live near Superfund National Priority hazardous waste sites have protested that the EPA is too concerned with saving money for the companies that pay for the cleanups, at the expense of the health and well-being of people living near the contaminated sites.

At one Superfund site at 1805 South Bannock Street in Denver, Colorado, for example, the EPA opted for a cleanup plan where the contaminated soil was treated and left onsite, instead of one where the contaminants were removed and transported to a licensed hazardous waste facility. Specifically, the contaminated soil—which was polluted with heavy metals and radioactive substances—was mixed with concrete and ash and the hardened product was placed back into the ground. The Shattuck Chemical Company, which was responsible for the original contamination on the site, paid an estimated $26 million for this cleanup. Removing the waste entirely, on the other hand, would have cost an estimated $37 million to $49 million.

Members of a neighborhood group called CLEANIT protested vigorously that this cleanup was insufficient, and that the cleanup plan which left contamination onsite was chosen simply because it would save the Shattuck Chemical Company money. In particular, people living in the neighborhood noticed that the contaminated cement rocks were sinking at an alarming rate. "That's supposed to last 2000 years," one resident told an Associated Press reporter, "but if it can't make it through one or two years, I don't know what's going to happen."[26]

Because of residents' protests, the site was reexamined by an independent firm. After an investigation, the firm agreed with the views of those living near the site, concluding that "the EPA failed to address long-term effects, the extent of groundwater contamination and possible runoff into the nearby South Platte River,"[27] according to a September 22, 1999, Associated Press (AP) report. The EPA has since agreed to revisit the site and it now appears likely that the EPA will decide in favor of offsite disposal. Denver, Colorado, is just one of many places where Superfund cleanups have been criticized as inadequate.

## Who pays for cleanups?

While environmentalists and residents living near contaminated sites are concerned that Superfund cleanups sometimes place the interests of the companies responsible for the contamination ahead of the interests of the public, business groups have taken a very different stance. These groups routinely object to the amount of money which companies responsible for contamination can be forced to pay toward cleaning up an abandoned hazardous waste

site. The Superfund law gives the president and EPA broad powers to collect money from companies connected to contaminated sites. Under Superfund, for example, any group of companies involved significantly in the dumping of hazardous wastes on a site can be made to pay the entire cost of cleanup, even if they are not responsible for absolutely all of the waste. Legally, this model of responsibility is called "joint and several liability."

Many companies oppose this legal framework, objecting to the fact that they could in theory be made to pay for the cleanup of more contamination than they themselves left behind. Mike Sweeney, head of a gold mining operation near Sutter Creek, California, expresses a typical view: "It's whoever has the deepest pocket is the one that's going to pay for it."[28] Some have proposed that Superfund's joint and several liability structure be changed to a framework where each company can be legally forced to pay, at a maximum, an amount toward cleanup that reflects the exact amount of contamination abandoned by the company.

*Rocks cover radioactive waste at the Shattuck Chemical Company in Denver, Colorado.*

For many environmentalists and for the EPA, however, an end to Superfund's joint and several liability structure is fraught with problems. On hazardous waste sites such as landfills, where many companies dumped varying amounts of hazardous waste, it is extremely difficult and often impossible to determine which chemical dumped by which company is responsible for what amount of contamination. Many of the hazardous waste sites today were contaminated twenty, thirty, or even fifty years ago, and few records exist to show exactly what happened during those years. The joint and several liability arrangement of Superfund places the EPA in a powerful bargaining position when it seeks payment for cleanup from the companies involved in contaminating such a site. Companies have less room for the legal maneuvering which one environmental lobbyist in the early 1980s called "legal buck-passing"[29]—trying to avoid paying part or most of the cleanup costs. Without joint and several liability, companies could in theory postpone payment for years by taking the EPA to court and arguing over the details of exactly how much waste each

*EPA testing and cleanups, such as this one at Love Canal, are costly. Determining who will pay for them is an ongoing problem.*

company dumped. It seems likely that the EPA, in order to complete a settlement, would then have to settle for companies paying even less than their fair share of the cleanup. Already, companies often take cleanup cases to court in an attempt to postpone payment, and the EPA sometimes settles out of court with companies for only a portion of the total cleanup amount.

Companies have placed significant pressure on the government to change Superfund's strict joint and several liability structure, and certain members of Congress who support the views of these companies have come close to passing amendments which would eliminate joint and several liability. In an effort to head off such a change, the EPA has recently promoted several compromise policies. For example, if the EPA believes that the companies paying for cleanup are not entirely responsible for contaminating a hazardous waste site, the EPA can voluntarily pay a certain amount, called "orphan shares," to make up the difference. In recent years, the EPA has increased the amount of money it puts toward orphan shares, paying an estimated $145 million from 1996 through 1998 so that companies could pay less. Furthermore, the EPA currently allows companies responsible for less than 1 percent of contamination to pay a small fee in keeping with their minor role in contamination, and then releases these companies from responsibility. The EPA also typically excuses companies altogether when their waste accounts for only a tiny fraction of contamination.

The EPA therefore does not always use its legal right under Superfund to make companies responsible for contamination pay the full cost of cleanup. However, environmentalists and the EPA believe that this right is a crucial part of the Superfund law. It places the EPA in a position to force a reasonable settlement with companies. Because of Superfund's joint and several liability structure, along with several other broad powers which Superfund gives to the EPA, the EPA has been able to collect approximately 70 percent—or about two-thirds—of the money for long-term cleanups from the companies legally responsible for contaminating sites. The other 30 percent of cleanup costs has been paid by the government. If Super-fund's joint and several liability arrangement were weakened, the EPA might collect even less than this partial percentage of cleanup costs.

## Brownfields and state cleanup programs

So far, the EPA has placed approximately fifteen hundred hazardous waste sites on its National Priority list for cleanup. At a conservative estimate, however, there are at least nine-teen thousand to twenty-two thousand severely contaminated sites scattered across the country. Including less contaminated sites, there are estimated to be more than one hundred thou-sand hazardous waste sites in the United States, not counting sites contaminated by leaking underground gasoline storage tanks. The EPA's Superfund program therefore addresses only a fraction of the nation's contaminated sites. The majority of contaminated sites are handled instead by state government programs. All fifty states now have their own hazardous waste cleanup programs, and altogether these state programs are cleaning up significantly more sites than the national Super-fund program. State governments therefore play a central role in the cleanup of the nation's hazardous waste sites.

In recent years, states have turned their focus toward hazardous waste sites called "brownfields." The typical brownfield is an abandoned industrial site in the city. Many cities have hundreds of brownfield hazardous waste sites. There are an estimated seven hundred brownfields in Cleveland, while roughly two thousand are scattered across the landscape of Chicago. With the current eco-nomic revival of many cities in the United States, there is considerable pressure to build new businesses, factories, and homes on these abandoned sites. Under this pressure, some states are changing the focus of their hazardous waste cleanup policies from those designed to assure that each site is completely cleaned up to policies whose pri-mary thrust is to speed up the redevelopment of these sites so that they can be bought and sold on the market.

Ohio is one of many states that has shifted its hazardous waste policies to favor the development of brownfields. In

1991, Ohio governor George Voinovich appointed a special Urban Industrial Property Revitalization Task Force to look into ways that laws might be changed to speed up this development. The task force produced a report titled *Removing the Barriers to the Redevelopment of Ohio's Abandoned Urban Industrial Property*. In response to this report, Ohio legislators passed a bill altering its hazardous waste cleanup law to promote the redevelopment of brownfields.

In particular, Ohio legislators weakened the standards for the cleanup of sites where companies plan to build a new industrial facility—reasoning that a place where people work can be left with more hazardous waste onsite than a place where people live. Ohio legislators also decided to offer a voluntary cleanup program. Under this program, if the owner of contaminated property voluntarily cleans up the property to meet certain standards, this owner is released from any legal obligation to perform additional investigation or cleanup should the state later decide that more cleanup is necessary. The Ohio Steel Industry Advisory

*Abandoned urban industrial sites, like this one, are known as brownfields. Such sites are often contaminated with hazardous waste.*

*A brownfield in Detroit. Many cities are striving to clean up and redevelop their brownfields.*

Council and the National Association of Realtors are two of the many business groups that support Ohio's new hazardous waste laws. In a statement before the House of Representatives Commerce Committee, a representative of the Ohio Steel Industry Advisory Council praised Ohio's programs as "an effort to stimulate the redevelopment of commercial and industrial sites."[30] Ohio is not the only state where brownfield development programs have been launched. Legislators in Indiana and New York, among other states, have adopted similar initiatives.

At the federal level, the EPA has also embraced brownfield redevelopment. To speed up the development of contaminated brownfields, the EPA has removed approximately thirty thousand sites from the list of those slated for potential Superfund cleanup—insisting that all of these sites have been thoroughly inspected and do not meet the level of contamination necessary to qualify as Superfund National Priority sites. The EPA also offers grants of up to $200,000 to help finance brownfield development. As of 1998, the EPA had awarded 227 of these grants.

State and federal governments have embraced brownfield redevelopment programs as a way to accelerate the cleanup and reuse of contaminated sites. Many major environmental groups, however, including Greenpeace and the Environmental Research Foundation, are concerned that, under these new brownfield programs, thousands of hazardous waste sites will be redeveloped with significant levels of hazardous waste contamination still onsite. Rena Steinzer, the director of the environmental law clinic at the University of Maryland, expresses a representative view: "In some state statutes, this streamlining of regulations has meant that developers get to choose the level of cleanup standards they meet. That makes me very uncomfortable, because state officials should be firmly in control of the level of cleanup."[31]

Neighborhood groups have also expressed concerns over the push for brownfield development. Although residents in working-class urban communities would very much like to see the development of the abandoned sites that stand neglected in their neighborhoods, community groups object to being left out of the decision-making process. Charles Lee, research director of the United Church of Christ Commission on Racial Justice, told environmental writer Steve Lerner the problem with the EPA's brownfield program: "The EPA's brownfield initiative was a locomotive that left the station without a major group of passengers aboard, and those are the folks struggling for environmental justice and the residents who live in the impacted communities."[32] Lerner adds, "Environmental justice advocates argue that the brownfields program cannot bring genuine environmental and economic improvements unless it is community driven."[33] Today, neighborhood groups are working hard to gain more control over brownfield decisions so that their concerns are addressed. Neighborhood groups balance the goals of real estate developers and industries by pushing for solutions that value the long-term health and well-being of the people in the neighborhood first and foremost.

## Cleaning up hazardous waste sites today

Today, the public's attention is no longer clearly focused on the problem of hazardous waste, and, under pressure from industry and business groups, the government's commitment to cleaning up hazardous waste sites has wavered. The Superfund program is facing serious political trouble. In 1995, Congress suspended the special taxes on crude oil and certain chemicals, and the special environmental taxes on business that finance the Superfund trust fund. Since that time, Superfund monies dwindled to $2.1 billion by 1998 and are expected to decrease to $1.3 billion by the end of 1999. To the dismay of environmentalists, some in Congress are talking of retiring Superfund as it slowly runs out of money. Meanwhile, some states have changed the emphasis of their hazardous waste cleanup programs, loosening environmental and legal standards to promote the development of contaminated sites. Preliminary investigation suggests that sites are getting cleaned up at a faster pace because of these changes. However, many are concerned that environmental issues are taking second place to the interests of industries and land developers. A recent report issued by the U.S. General Accounting Office (GAO) explained: "Since the state practices can reduce cleanup costs, they are generally advantageous for businesses and others responsible for cleaning the sites."[34]

In the face of these trends, environmental and neighborhood groups nevertheless continue to fight for the cleanup of the many thousands of hazardous waste sites marking the American rural and urban landscape. Thanks to their efforts, hazardous waste sites in the United States are getting cleaned up. At the same time, EPA head Carol Browner is working to have the taxes for Superfund reinstated, ending the "tax holiday"[35] for companies, as she has called it, and allowing her agency to move ahead with the cleanup efforts begun more than two decades ago by the activism of Lois Gibbs, Debbie Cerrillo, and other residents of Niagara Falls.

# 4

# Radioactive Waste

SURROUNDED BY THE farmland of southeastern Washington State, the Hanford Nuclear Reservation stands as an example of the problems which radioactive waste can cause. From 1943 to 1989, the U.S. government used the Hanford Reservation to manufacture plutonium for the production of nuclear bombs. Hanford's operations relied upon the use of radioactive materials, and as a result the facility generated millions of gallons of radioactive waste. As early as the 1950s, at least some of Hanford's radioactive waste was released directly into the Columbia River, which runs alongside of the facility. Another 54 million gallons of highly radioactive waste was poured into 177 underground tanks buried onsite. Most of the tanks were single-shelled—only one layer of metal lay between the waste and the ground. Today, sixty-seven of these tanks are leaking. More than one million gallons of radioactive waste have seeped into the ground, and some of this waste has begun to contaminate groundwater, flowing with this groundwater toward the Columbia River. In a March 1998 public television broadcast of the *Lehrer News Hour,* Mike Wilson, head of the nuclear waste division in the Washington State Department of Ecology, explained the situation. "Once this material is in the water it is almost impossible to retrieve it from the water," he said, "so the stuff that is now in the groundwater is going to go on towards the river."[36] More than 120,000 people count on the Columbia as a source of drinking water.

*A cooling tower at Washington's Hanford Nuclear Reservation, one of the most contaminated radioactive waste sites in the United States.*

According to the U.S. General Accounting Office (GAO), "the Hanford site . . . has one of the greatest concentrations of radioactive waste in the world," and cleanup of the site "is a very costly, complex, and risky effort."[37] The situation at Hanford is therefore recognized as a serious environmental problem. The Hanford Reservation, however, is only one of many places in the United States now contaminated with radioactive waste.

## What is radioactive waste?

Radioactive waste is waste that contains radioactive elements, or that has come into contact with radioactive elements and therefore becomes contaminated. Radioactive elements change over time into other substances through a process called decay. As these elements decay, they send out nuclear particles as radiation. Commonly, radioactive elements regularly emit (give off) either two protons and two neutrons together, called "alpha" radiation, or one electron, called "beta" radiation. Many of the radioactive elements that release beta radiation also emit very high energy photons called "gamma" radiation.

Radioactive elements emit less radiation as time passes, ultimately decaying into nonradioactive matter. Certain types of radioactive elements lose most of their radioactivity in a matter of hours, while others continue to emit radiation for thousands or even millions of years. Common radioactive elements used by people today include uranium and plutonium.

Exposure to radioactive waste can cause serious illness because radiation damages cells and the DNA inside cells. Exposure to radiation can cause a variety of cancers, as well as damage to internal organs and the immune system. It can also cause radiation poisoning, the symptoms of which include nausea, fatigue, sores, loss of hair, and loss of teeth.

According to the United States Department of Energy (DOE), there are currently more than 145 million cubic meters of radioactive waste in the United States. Much of this radioactive waste has been generated by three activities: the government's production of nuclear weapons, private utility companies' use of nuclear power plants to generate electricity, and uranium mining. A very small amount of radioactive waste is also generated by hospitals and the health care industry, since certain medical procedures, such as radiation therapy for the treatment of cancer, use radioactive substances. Under federal laws, the handling and disposal of most radioactive waste is regulated by a government body called the Nuclear Regulatory Commission (NRC).

## Uranium mining

The production of nuclear weapons and the operation of nuclear power plants both rely on the radioactive substance uranium, a rare radioactive metal found in the earth. Thus, industrial activities involving radioactive substances typically begin with the mining of uranium. In the United States, uranium mines are found mostly in the southwestern states.

Uranium mines have created a serious environmental problem because they generate a significant amount of radioactive waste. Uranium mining companies leave behind enormous piles of radioactive waste called uranium tailings, a fine, sandy rock containing uranium. Uranium mines in the United States have so far generated more than 118 million cubic meters of this sandy radioactive waste. One example of this waste can be found on the banks of the Colorado River near Moab, Utah. There, a now-bankrupt company called the Atlas Corporation has left 10.5 million tons of uranium tailings covering 150 acres and rising as high as forty feet.

## The manufacture of nuclear weapons

Uranium mining is just one of the industries that generates a significant amount of radioactive waste. The production of nuclear weapons, conducted by the United States government, is another activity that has generated significant amounts of radioactive waste. To date, the production of nuclear weapons has generated more than one million cubic meters of waste. Approximately 350,000 cubic meters of this waste is highly radioactive waste, which emits extremely high levels of radiation.

Overall, the United States government has done a poor job of managing and disposing of this radioactive waste. In particular, the DOE—the agency charged with overseeing nuclear weapons facilities—and the various private contractors which the DOE has hired over the years to run its nuclear weapons plants have failed to protect the public and the environment from radioactive contamination. Former DOE Secretary of Energy Admiral James D. Watkins acknowledged in 1989 that the DOE was part of "a 40-year culture cloaked in secrecy and imbued with a dedication to the production of nuclear weapons without a real sensitivity for protecting the environment."[38]

There are eighteen major facilities in thirteen states used by the United States government for the manufacture of nuclear weapons, and almost all of these facilities either have had their grounds contaminated with radioactive waste or have contaminated surrounding towns, land, or waterways. At the government's Fernald plant eighteen miles northwest of Cincinnati, Ohio, for example—where uranium was processed for weapons production—operators illegally dumped more than 109 million gallons of waste contaminated with radiation into sewers. At another uranium processing plant in Paducah, Kentucky, reports only recently surfaced, due in part to investigative work done by Joby Warrick of the *Washington Post,* that operators recklessly washed radioactive waste into ditches draining off of the site, and dumped radioactive garbage in an area north of the plant.

Severe radioactive waste contamination was also discovered at the government's Rocky Flats nuclear facility in Colorado, where operators produced plutonium triggers for nuclear warheads. In a statement made in 1992, a grand jury in Colorado described the events surrounding this discovery: "When agents of the Federal Bureau of Investigation [FBI] and the Environmental Protection Agency [EPA] raided the [Rocky Flats] plant on June 6, 1989, they found compelling evidence that hazardous wastes and radioactive mixed wastes had been illegally stored, treated, and disposed of . . . at the plant in violation of the Resource Conservation and Recovery Act [RCRA]. These agents also discovered violations of the Clean Water Act and other environmental statutes through a variety of continuing acts, including the illegal discharge of pollutants, hazardous materials, and radioactive matter into the Platte River, Woman Creek, Walnut Creek, and the drinking water supplies for the cities of Broomfield and Westminster, Colorado."[39] Rockwell International, the contractor hired by the DOE to operate Rocky Flats, was ultimately fined $18.5 million after admitting to five felony charges.

The public will be paying for the cleanup of the government's nuclear weapons facilities for years to come. The cost of cleanup at the Washington State Hanford Nuclear Reservation alone has been estimated at $50 billion to $57 billion. The cleanup of all DOE facilities is expected to cost an incredible $240 billion.

*Maintenance workers at the Rocky Flats nuclear facility in Colorado clean the walls of radioactive waste.*

## Nuclear power plants

The production of electricity using nuclear power is another activity responsible for generating large amounts of radioactive waste. The first commercial nuclear power plant opened in 1958 in Shippingport, Pennsylvania, at a time when nuclear power was hailed by many as the solution to the country's need for electricity. Five years earlier, then-president Dwight D. Eisenhower had declared that by harnessing atomic energy for peaceful aims, "this greatest of destructive forces can be developed into a great boon for the benefit of all mankind."[40] A year after Eisenhower's declaration, the chairman of the U.S. Atomic Energy Commission, Lewis Strauss, proclaimed that, due to the future use of nuclear power plants to generate electricity, "it is not too much to expect that our children will enjoy in their homes electrical energy too cheap to meter."[41]

Nuclear power plants have not lived up to this promise, however. Utility companies are no longer building nuclear power plants, and many of the existing plants are expected to close in upcoming years. Today, there are 103 private nuclear power plants operating in the United States, most of them in the eastern part of the country. So far, twenty nuclear power plants in the United States have permanently closed.

Nuclear power plants generate a significant amount of radioactive waste. In particular, they have so far generated more than 700,000 cubic meters of low-level radioactive waste—waste which emits small amounts of radiation. Low-level radioactive waste from nuclear power plants includes metal objects, clothing, and other materials that have become contaminated with radiation through exposure to radioactive substances. This waste is typically shipped to special disposal facilities licensed to handle such materials. In the future, nuclear power plants are expected to generate enormous amounts of low-level radioactive waste as they close down, in the form of cement, scrap metal, and objects once used at the facility.

Nuclear power plants also generate a large amount of highly radioactive waste, in the form of used radioactive fuel,

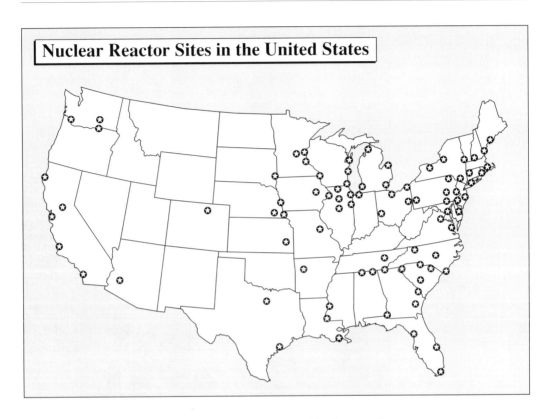

**Nuclear Reactor Sites in the United States**

called "spent fuel." Spent fuel, typically encased in long rods, contains the radioactive substances uranium and plutonium. Nuclear power plants have already generated approximately 13,700 cubic meters of this waste, and they produce approximately 1,900 tons of new radioactive spent fuel each year.

## The disposal of high-level waste

Spent fuel from nuclear power plants is one example of highly radioactive waste, called "high-level waste." Another example of high-level waste is the liquid residue left over from the government's production of nuclear weapons. One of the most controversial issues surrounding the disposal of radioactive waste is the question of where to dispose of these high-level wastes. At present, there is no place designed to accept high-level wastes for permanent disposal. This is due to the fact that, according to guidelines set by the Nuclear Regulatory Commission (NRC), high-level wastes must be kept from entering the public water supply

*A nuclear power plant cooling tower. Nuclear power plants produce thousands of cubic meters of radioactive waste each year.*

for at least one thousand years, and disposed wastes must pose no unreasonable risk to public safety. Further, a high-level waste disposal site is supposed to endure for ten thousand years. No disposal site has so far met these standards.

Despite the fact that there has never been a place to dispose of high-level radioactive wastes, both the government and private utility companies have been generating high-level wastes for decades. At present the government and utility companies are storing these wastes temporarily. Most spent fuel generated by the commercial nuclear power industry is stored at the nuclear power plants themselves, either in large pools of water or above ground in gigantic, forty-foot-high containers called dry casks. Most of the government's high-level waste is stored in underground tanks in three locations: the DOE Hanford Reservation in southern Washington State, the DOE Savannah River plant in South Carolina, and the DOE Idaho National Engineering Laboratories. Since the DOE and the nuclear power industry are both saddled with enormous amounts of high-level wastes, they both favor the opening of a permanent disposal site which would accept these wastes.

In 1982, the United States government began a serious search for a place to put high-level waste. In that year, Congress passed the Nuclear Waste Policy Act (NWPA), which charged the DOE itself with the task of finding a place for the long-term disposal of this waste. Congress initially recommended that two sites be chosen for disposal, and the DOE planned to choose one site in the eastern United States and one in the West. This arrangement would have meant that wastes shipped from power plants and government facilities to a disposal site would travel shorter distances, and therefore there would be less risk of an accident during transportation. However, the DOE soon abandoned plans for investigating a site in the East and decided to choose only one site for disposal, in the western United States. According to Paul Gunter, environmentalist and director of the Reactor Watchdog Project based in Washington, D.C., the DOE abandoned plans for a disposal site in the East because there were political concerns that people in the eastern United States would become less accepting of nuclear power plants—most of which operate in the East—if the waste generated by those plants were left permanently somewhere in the region.

In 1986, the DOE proposed looking into three possible permanent high-level waste disposal sites: Hanford, Washington; Deaf Smith County, Texas; and Yucca Mountain, Nevada. The DOE recommended that each of these sites be investigated to decide which one was most suitable as a disposal site. However, in 1987, Congress voted that only the Yucca Mountain site be considered. Yucca Mountain is located on federally owned land, twelve miles north of the

*The proposed Yucca Mountain, Nevada, nuclear waste disposal facility. This site is being investigated as a potential disposal site for the nation's high-level radioactive waste.*

nearest homes and approximately one hundred miles northwest of Las Vegas, Nevada.

Since 1987, the DOE has therefore had the task of investigating Yucca Mountain, Nevada, to see whether it is a suitable site for the permanent disposal of high-level radioactive waste. Currently, the DOE is considering a plan that proposes placing the waste in containers and burying it beneath Yucca Mountain at a depth of one thousand feet, in chambers spreading over fifteen hundred acres. If the DOE decides that this plan meets NRC guidelines, it will submit the plan to the NRC. The NRC, along with the EPA, will then judge whether Yucca Mountain meets all necessary environmental regulations. If Yucca Mountain is approved, millions of cubic meters of high-level waste will be shipped to the site over the course of thirty or forty years. If Yucca Mountain is not approved, high-level waste will remain in temporary storage across the country. Approximately 75 to 80 percent of people living in Nevada oppose the Yucca Mountain site, many of them outraged that Nevada may become the dumping ground for high-level radioactive waste that nobody else in the country wants.

## Geology of Yucca Mountain

There are several characteristics which a suitable site must exhibit to meet with approval. The geology of the site should be stable and unlikely to change for at least ten thousand years. Groundwater movement on the site should be slow, so that radioactive waste cannot quickly move away from the site into public water supplies. Also, the site should be remote and far from major population centers. The DOE claims that Yucca Mountain fulfills all of these characteristics, according to preliminary research conducted by DOE scientists. However, since the DOE is currently holding a significant amount of high-level waste, it has reasons to support the approval of the Yucca Mountain disposal plans. For this reason, environmentalists and some scientists are skeptical that the DOE's investigation of the site has been objective.

In particular, researchers working for the Nevada state government, which opposes the plan, have called DOE's site managers and contractors overly optimistic. According to Nevada state researchers, who have carefully watched DOE scientists and workers as they investigate Yucca Mountain, "Potentially disqualifying conditions [for approval of Yucca Mountain as a high-level waste disposal

*A Yucca Mountain worker walks down the facility's main tunnel. The DOE maintains that the site is geologically sound, but others claim that it may be unstable.*

site] . . . do, in fact, exist at Yucca Mountain."[42] For example, fractures have been found in the rock formations of Yucca Mountain where none were initially expected. Groundwater is expected to move quickly through these fractures, which means that radioactive waste may be carried away from the site and into public water supplies well before one thousand years have passed. Certain geologic formations within Yucca Mountain also suggest that hot water may swell up from beneath the mountain, causing a release of radioactive waste both into the air and away from the site with groundwater. Moreover, since 1976, more than six hundred earthquake tremors of magnitude greater than 2.5 have occurred within fifty miles of Yucca Mountain, including a magnitude 5.6 earthquake which struck just ten miles southeast of the site in 1992. A major earthquake could change the geology of the disposal site, shifting water levels. Thus, Yucca Mountain may not be stable enough to qualify as a well-suited disposal site.

Scientists working with the DOE have dismissed these concerns as unfounded, however. "Our modeling is over-conservative," insists Abraham E. Van Luik, policy advisor for performance assessment at the site. "Absolutely nobody is going to get hurt by this repository for hundreds of thousands of years."[43]

Contradicting Luik's claims, though, is a report released by a scientific peer review panel sponsored by the DOE itself. The panel was critical of the DOE's current research into the site, and concluded that determining what will happen to waste buried at Yucca Mountain "may be beyond the analytical capabilities of any scientific and engineering team."[44] The panel felt that it may be impossible for scientists today to forecast the future for radioactive waste buried inside Yucca Mountain. If it is true that scientists cannot predict what will happen to the radioactive waste, then the proposed plan for disposal at Yucca Mountain may not meet the NRC's public safety guidelines.

As the scientific argument over Yucca Mountain rages on, environmentalists fear that, since Yucca Mountain is the only site under consideration, pressure to do something with the waste will oblige the DOE to select the site, even without firm scientific evidence that Yucca Mountain is safe. If Yucca Mountain is not approved, it could take several decades more to find another site for disposal—since the DOE is not currently researching any alternatives. Despite the potential for a long wait, however, many believe that a hasty decision should not be made now since it could affect people living in America for thousands of years to come. Dr. Allison Macfarlane from Harvard University's Kennedy School of Government expressed a typical view to a *New York Times* reporter: "We shouldn't be rushing the process. . . . We should make sure we get it right."[45]

## Transportation risks associated with Yucca Mountain site

Besides the risks associated with the quick spread of contamination from the Yucca Mountain site, the plan for disposal at Yucca Mountain poses another danger: the risk of an accident during the transportation of high-level waste from power plants and government facilities to the mountain. Although the DOE has internally evaluated the risks associated with transportation accidents, it has not released details on proposed transportation routes or schedules. According to the State of Nevada, though, DOE maps show that much of the radioactive waste will likely pass through the county of Las Vegas; some of it may even pass through the city of Las Vegas itself. Moreover, Nevada is not the only state that will be affected by the transportation of high-level waste to Yucca Mountain. Since the proposed disposal site would accept waste from across the country, high-level waste would be transported through forty-three states. According to a careful analysis of the DOE's transportation plan conducted by the State of Nevada Agency for Nuclear Projects, an average of one truck of radioactive waste a day for thirty-nine years may be transported through San Bernardino County in California, and as much as 75 percent of the waste shipments to Yucca Mountain will likely travel through Illinois, some of it passing close to Chicago.

## Recycling radioactive waste into consumer products

The Yucca Mountain debate is just one of many controversies centering on the disposal of radioactive waste. Recently, a new controversy over radioactive waste has emerged in the United States—this one over the recycling of low-level radioactive waste. As nuclear power plants and government nuclear facilities shut down, much of the equipment, machinery, and concrete from these facilities qualify as low-level waste—since these materials have become contaminated with radiation. The EPA estimates that nuclear facilities will generate as much as six hundred thousand tons of contaminated metal alone in upcoming years.

Specially designed disposal sites are available in the United States to accept this waste. However, in an effort to save money on disposal, nuclear facilities are looking toward a controversial new practice: the recycling of radioactive scrap metal into metal used for consumer goods, such as pots and pans, metal toys, kitchen appliances, and lamps.

Today, the NRC is already allowing this recycling to take place. In particular, the DOE has a contract with the company BNFL, Inc., to remove all equipment and materials from the DOE's Oak Ridge Tennesee nuclear facility, and BNFL is selling some of the contaminated metal from the Oak Ridge facility to metal companies. The metal companies, in turn, are melting the radioactive metal so that it can be mixed with regular metal. Proud of its efforts to recycle this radioactive metal, the DOE Oak Ridge facility announced in a Vision 2010 statement—describing its goals for the year 2010—that the "DOE expects to save $9 billion over the cost of disposal through these recycling efforts."[46] Although nobody knows exactly where the radioactive metal being recycled today will end up—since there is currently no rule stating that radioactive metal be labeled as such—it could appear mixed into any consumer product, including cars, frying pans, silverware, zippers, and in construction materials such as the girders in bridges and buildings.

At present, the recycling of radioactive scrap metal can only happen on a case-by-case basis, if the NRC gives special approval. The DOE received this approval for its contract with BNFL, Inc. The NRC is now moving ahead with plans to streamline the recycling process, however, and has proposed setting standard limits for radiation in consumer goods so that it need not examine individual requests for recycling. The highest of the three limits being considered would allow people in the United States to be exposed to the equivalent of one chest x ray a year—10 millirems—through radiation emitted by objects in their homes, businesses, or surroundings. The NRC believes that, if limits are set low enough, public health will not be put at risk.

However, a wide range of environmental, consumer, and nuclear watchdog groups concerned with the environmental impact of radioactive waste oppose this practice. Most agree

*Tennessee's Oak Ridge nuclear facility (pictured) recycles its radioactive scrap metal into metal sold to the public.*

that recycling radioactive wastes will put the public at risk. According to the consumer organization Public Citizen, the environmental group Greenpeace, the nuclear watchdog group Nuclear Information & Resource Service (NIRS), and others, "Using radioactive wastes in consumer products poses unnecessary, avoidable, involuntary, uninformed risks."[47] The Steel Manufacturers Association has also weighed in against this controversial practice, concerned that its own products will become contaminated. In an interview with *San Francisco Examiner* correspondent Erin McCormick, Tom Danjczek, president of the association, explained: "When you get in your car or use a spoon, you don't want to have to think about whether it's contaminated with radioactivity or not."[48]

Many of these organizations do not believe that the limits for radiation exposure proposed by the NRC are safe. "I don't think the American public is going to want to buy products that give them the equivalent of an extra chest x ray every year," explains Dan Hirsch, president of the environmental group Committee to Bridge the Gap. "They're talking about giving you 70 extra chest x rays in your lifetime. I don't think that's acceptable."[49] Nor do concerned organizations trust that, once radiation is allowed in consumer goods, there will be any reasonable way to know how much radiation each product emits, or how much a given person is exposed to—facts that would depend on the different types of radioactive products surrounding the person. "It is not credible to believe computer models can calculate and accurately predict any or ALL of the doses to the public and the environment from all of the potential radioactivity that could be released over time,"[50] explains a statement issued by the Nuclear Information & Resource Service, Public Citizen, and other organizations.

## Protesting against radioactive waste recycling

Many of the groups opposing the recycling of radioactive scrap metal believe that public protest and vigilant scrutiny of the process are the only actions that can put a halt to the recycling that has already begun. In one report titled "The Floodgates Are Opening For Radioactive Metal

Recycling!" the public interest group Public Citizen explains that they are "organizing a large grassroots response" and asking people to "Get involved today!"[51] Meanwhile, the Nuclear Information & Resource Service provides a sample letter about the issue on its website for people to copy and mail to the NRC. On August 11, 1999, these two groups and 248 others sent a letter to Vice President Al Gore expressing their extreme concern over the recycling already happening in Oak Ridge, Tennessee.

In part due to this pressure, DOE Secretary Bill Richardson announced in January 2000 that the DOE would temporarily halt the recycling of certain types of radioactively contaminated metal—those metals contaminated throughout with radiation. However, the DOE continues to recycle metal contaminated on the surface with radiation. Public Citizen immediately reacted to the DOE's new stance by stating that the DOE's adjusted plan falls far short of protecting the public, and environmental groups have continued their protests. These groups are trying to get the word out to the public, concerned that people are unaware that radioactive scrap metal is already being recycled into consumer goods.

# 5

# Incineration, Recycling, and Reduction

THERE ARE ALTERNATIVES to the disposal of hazardous wastes on land, or in rivers, lakes, and other bodies of water. For example, companies have turned increasingly to the incineration (burning) of their hazardous wastes. When done correctly, incineration can destroy close to 100 percent of some synthetic toxic chemicals.

The incineration of hazardous waste is done using extremely hot industrial ovens, and the temperature of these ovens must not be allowed to fall below a certain level if incineration is to be successful. If an industrial plant already uses very hot ovens as a part of its manufacturing process, the plant will sometimes use these same ovens to burn its hazardous wastes. If a facility does not operate ovens at high enough temperatures, the facility will sometimes send its waste to other industrial plants that do operate ovens hot enough for incineration. Companies that bake limestone and shale or clay into cement, for example, are often allowed to accept and burn hazardous wastes from other facilities. A significant portion of hazardous waste incineration is therefore done at existing industrial plants. Special hazardous waste incinerators are also sometimes built for the sole purpose of burning wastes.

Since the destruction of wastes is preferable to their disposal on land or in water, incineration may appear at first glance to be a solution to the problem. However, incineration cannot destroy all hazardous wastes. Heavy metals, for example, cannot be eliminated by burning. Incineration is therefore useful only for addressing the disposal of certain wastes, and cannot serve as an alternative to hazardous waste disposal in general.

## Incineration of waste brings its own environmental problems

Besides this fundamental limitation, incineration also brings with it another problem. Incinerators create pollution. In particular, when incinerators burn hazardous wastes, they send toxic chemicals into the air through their smokestacks. Hazardous waste incinerators therefore turn the problem of land and water pollution into one of air pollution. Among the toxins typically released by hazardous waste incinerators are the toxic chemical dioxin and the heavy metal mercury. Both dioxin and mercury are of primary concern because of the health effects associated with exposure to even small amounts of these chemicals.

Because of the air pollution associated with hazardous waste incinerators, residents often strongly object to the placement of an incinerator in their town or city. People do not want to be exposed to airborne toxic chemicals any more than they wish to be exposed to toxic chemicals in water, food, or soil. All over the country, people have protested against the construction of hazardous waste incinerators in their communities, and in some cases they have won. In Lewiston, New York, for example, residents fought hard to stop construction of two incinerators proposed by the hazardous waste disposal company Chemical Waste Management (CWM). Environmental lawyer Michael Gerrard, who represented the residents of Lewiston, recalls the reason for their struggle in his book *Whose Backyard, Whose Risk*. "At community meetings there was palpable fear about the danger the incinerators would cause to the community and, especially, to its children," Gerrard explains. "Mothers demanded, but could not be given, absolute guarantees that their sons and daughters would not get cancer from the emissions."[52] With Gerrard's help, the residents of Lewiston were ultimately successful, and CWM's proposed incinerators were not built.

Hazardous waste incinerators pose the immediate threat of air pollution to the people who live near them. However, they also have an environmental impact well beyond the borders of nearby towns. Dioxin, mercury, and other toxic chemicals released into the air by incinerators can travel very long distances, falling unseen onto land, lakes, and rivers far from the location of the incinerators. Some of the contamination in the Great Lakes, for example, comes from air pollution that has traveled from as far away as Texas. Thus, every new hazardous waste incinerator that is built—as well as every existing industrial plant which obtains a permit to burn hazardous waste in its own ovens—adds to the pollution problems of the nation as a whole. In particular, incinerators add to the levels of dioxin and mercury in the nation's waterways.

Nevertheless, the EPA maintains that the incineration of wastes is preferable to simple land disposal or releasing wastes into the nation's waterways; incineration does at least destroy certain hazardous wastes, even at the cost of

*Citizens protest the construction of a hazardous medical waste incinerator in their community.*

air pollution. Certain environmental groups agree that incineration—although extremely problematic—is nevertheless preferable to the simple land or surface water disposal of waste. However, for people living near a hazardous waste incinerator, incineration may be no more acceptable than the release of wastes into the land or water of their community, since the air pollution from incineration also threatens their health. For people in these communities, each hazardous waste incinerator is simply one more polluting facility added to the industrial landscape.

Regardless of the problems associated with hazardous waste incineration, the fact that incineration is only an option for certain hazardous waste limits its possibilities. At present only 9 percent of the hazardous waste generated by large manufacturing facilities is incinerated each year.

## Hazardous waste recycling

Another disposal alternative is recycling. Industrial solvents such as trichloroethylene (TCE), for example, are sometimes sent to "solvent recovery" facilities where the solvents are cleaned and redistributed for use. Hazardous ash containing heavy metals from steel mills and incinerators can sometimes be sent to metal recovery facilities that seperate the ash from the metals. The metals then can sometimes be sold for re-use. In one case of recycling on-site, an electronics firm that was using three separate solvents to clean machine parts, circuit boards, and computer housings switched to the use of one solvent instead, recycling it for each stage of cleaning. The single solvent was used first on the circuit boards, then on the housings, and finally on the machine parts. Not only did this reduce the amount of solvent used, but it left the firm with one solvent to dispose of in the end, instead of having a mixture of three solvents, which would have been much more difficult to treat or recycle.

Companies are encouraged to recycle their hazardous wastes whenever possible, instead of incinerating or disposing of wastes. Many hazardous wastes, however, cannot be recycled. Sometimes, the wastes are mixed together

too completely to be separated. Other wastes, such as dioxins, simply have no use. For these reasons and others, most hazardous wastes are not currently recycled. As of 1997, only 10 percent of the hazardous wastes generated by large manufacturing facilities were recycled.

## Recycling hazardous waste as fertilizer

Recycling hazardous waste is generally thought to be a positive trend. The pressure to find some way to reuse hazardous wastes, however, has led to some controversial recycling practices. In particular, certain hazardous wastes are now being mixed into commercial fertilizers and sold to farmers. For years, one steel mill in Norfolk, Nebraska, operated by a company called Nucor, took ash waste containing zinc, lead, and cadmium and mixed it into fertilizer, which was then sold to farmers. The James River Corporation, which operates a paper mill on the Columbia River in Camas, Washington, also has been known to recycle waste into fertilizer. On a monthly basis, approximately seven hundred tons of ash, containing zinc, lead, and cadmium, was removed from the paper mill chimney, mixed with water, and trucked to six farms in southern Washington State, where it was spread onto the fields. These mills were allowed to recycle their wastes as fertilizer in part because the wastes contained zinc. Zinc is a metal which, at certain levels, is considered beneficial to crops. The fact that the wastes also contained lead and cadmium was ignored, because the EPA believed that the crops did not absorb enough of these heavy metals to pose a threat to public health when the crops were eaten.

Environmental groups such as the Environmental Working Group of Washington, D.C., are extremely concerned with this type of recycling. Although crops may not absorb heavy metals—a fact which is disputed by certain scientific research, however, in the case of cadmium—the farmers who spread the contaminated fertilizer over their fields are at risk of exposure themselves, as are other adults, children, or animals which come into contact with the fertilizer after it is laid on the fields. Once the waste has been spread, moreover, rains can carry contamination into nearby waterways, and the farmland itself absorbs the waste over time. At least a few farmers have had their crops and land ruined by fertilizer contaminated with exceptionally high amounts of heavy metals. In Tifton, Georgia, for example, more than one thousand acres of valuable peanut crops died after they were treated with fertilizer containing waste from steel mills.

Environmentalists are particularly concerned by the fact that fertilizers containing hazardous wastes are not required to carry labels stating how much waste they contain, or even the fact that they do contain hazardous wastes. "The lack of national regulation and of labeling requirements means most farmers have no idea exactly what they're putting on their crops when they apply fertilizers,"[53] *Seattle Times* reporter Duff Wilson explained in one of a series of 1997 articles on the subject.

The EPA has set some limits for the amount and types of hazardous wastes which can be mixed with fertilizers, and certain states are now moving toward regulation of this controversial recycling practice. In the fall of 1999, the California Department of Food and Agriculture proposed strict limits on the amount of heavy metals allowed into the environment through fertilizers.

For environmental groups, however, government regulations have not gone far enough. In California, the public interest group CalPIRG and the Environmental Working Group have called for stricter limits than those suggested by the state, and demanded labeling requirements that would force fertilizer companies to disclose how much hazardous waste is contained in their fertilizer. Bill Walker, California director of the Environmental Working Group, explained in a press release: "At the very least, the label should inform consumers that the [fertilizer] product contains high levels of persistent toxins."[54]

Presently, a number of companies still sell fertilizer contaminated with hazardous waste. According to a November 18, 1999, report in the *San Francisco Examiner*, for example, there are at least eight companies selling fertilizer in California "that exceeded toxicity for lead, cadmium or arsenic under federal hazardous waste criteria . . . includ[ing] Ironite Products Co., Liquid Chemical Corp., Western Farm Service Inc., American Minerals, Bay Zinc Co., Britz Fertilizers Inc., Monterey Chemical Co. and Mineral King."[55]

## Reducing and eliminating hazardous wastes

As long as wastes continue to be generated, their disposal presents a serious problem with no obvious solution. For this reason, it is generally agreed that the best solution to the problem of hazardous waste is simply to generate less waste in the first place. Environmentalists have long tried to promote this principle—known as "source reduction"—calling for the use of alternative industrial practices that generate less waste. Environmentalists firmly believe in the ingenuity of businesses and maintain that companies can find ways to replace the use of hazardous chemicals.

Some companies have already embraced alternative practices. For example, a handful of dry cleaners across the country have turned entirely to "wet cleaning," which replaces the hazardous solvent perchloroethylene (perc) with other, nontoxic substitutes. Additionally, researchers at the Argonne National Laboratory, a research lab operated by the University of Chicago on behalf of the DOE, have developed an efficient way to mass-produce a biodegradable chemical called ethyl lactate, which they believe may serve

*The owner of a dry cleaning store demonstrates wet cleaning, which uses water-based cleaning solutions instead of perc.*

to replace many industrial solvents. Since industrial solvents have contaminated water supplies across the nation, their replacement with a less-toxic, easily biodegradable chemical such as ethyl lactate would be a major step toward the protection of public health.

## Present environmental laws favor pollution control over pollution prevention

Environmentalists see clear benefits to phasing out current industrial practices and replacing them with alternatives that generate less hazardous waste or no hazardous waste at all. However, environmental laws and policies continue to focus on controlling and regulating the amount of waste allowed into the environment instead of pushing for the reduction and elimination of hazardous waste altogether. As environmental engineer William C. Blackman explains in his book on hazardous waste management, the government's environmental policy approach "continues to be pollution control rather than pollution prevention."[56]

The Resource Conservation and Recovery Act (RCRA), for example, starts with bold words: "The Congress hereby declares it to be the national policy of the United States that, wherever feasible, the generation of hazardous waste is to be reduced or eliminated as expeditiously [promptly] as possible." However, RCRA is not a law focused on the elimination of waste. The next sentence of its policy statement reads, "Waste that is nevertheless generated should be treated, stored, or disposed of so as to minimize the present and future threat to human health and the environment."[57]

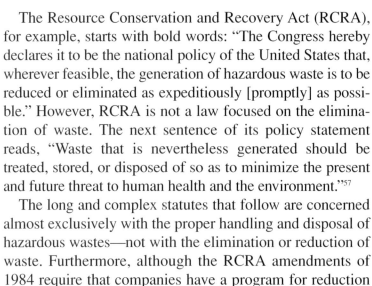

*A hazardous waste worker tests for dioxins. Some experts have argued the necessity of sunsetting organochlorines, the use of which add to dioxins in the environment.*

The long and complex statutes that follow are concerned almost exclusively with the proper handling and disposal of hazardous wastes—not with the elimination or reduction of waste. Furthermore, although the RCRA amendments of 1984 require that companies have a program for reduction in place, they do not specify how much reduction must take place or require companies to follow through on these programs. As a result, industries are not making serious strides toward reduction under this rule.

## Sunsetting organochlorines

Some government officials and environmental groups have called for much bolder policies than the regulatory ones currently in place—policies that would require industries to set and meet deadlines for the reduction and elimination of hazardous waste. The International Joint Commission (IJC), for example, a governmental body which includes representatives from both the United States and Canada, has called for the eventual phasing out, or "sunsetting," of a class of chemicals called organochlorines. Some of the most problematic hazardous wastes—including dioxins, polychlorinated biphenyls (PCBs), and trichloroethylene (TCE)—are organochlorines or by-products of organochlorines. Recognizing the environmental damage already caused by these chemicals, the IJC has come to the conclusion that industries should be required to put an end to their use.

> In his book The Making of a Conservative Environmentalist, the former United States chairman to the IJC, Republican politician Gordon K. Durnil, explains the reasons that the IJC has taken this stance: "I think anyone who has worked in government and has engaged in this troublesome issue of what to do about toxic substances has come to understand that the attempts to regulate such substances have not resulted in a terribly efficient or successful set of programs. . . . Regulatory standards tend to be excuses which enable governments to set exceptions for the discharge of various poisons into the waters of North America through the collection of fees and the issuance of permits. . . . So surely it is time to ask: do we really want to continue our attempts to manage persistent toxic substances, or . . . do we want to begin the process of eliminating such onerous [troublesome] substances in the first place? . . . By consensus, we [the IJC] made the decision that the health of humans was at risk. This decision fostered other decisions, such as the recommendations to sunset the most onerous of toxic substances."[58]

The IJC is only one of the groups to propose an end to the widespread use of organochlorines. In 1994, the American Public Health Association—an organization of fifty thousand public health workers—also came out in favor of sunsetting organochlorines instead of simply regulating the use of these chemicals as is currently done. "Elimination of chlorine and/or chlorinated organic compounds from certain manufacturing processes, products, and uses may be the most cost-effective and health-protective way to reduce health and environmental exposures to chlorinated organic compounds,"[59] the association concluded.

However, the chemical companies that manufacture organochlorines strongly object to the idea of sunsetting these chemicals, and have lobbied hard against any such regulations. Many of those in the chemical industry insist that the use of organochlorines is a positive trend. Chlorine "is such a valuable and useful molecule because it does so many things and is involved in so many end products,"[60] John Sesody, an executive from the chemical company Elf Atochem, told environmental writer Ivan Amato. Because many organochlorines have not been tested for toxicity, industry groups maintain that some of these chemicals may be harmless. Companies argue that each organochlorine should be tested before it is seriously restricted. Companies also maintain that the elimination of organochlorines may lead to the use of other untested, potentially harmful chemicals instead. Further, it is impractical to sunset organochlorines, they propose, since industry's use of these chemicals is so widespread.

However, the government has banned the use of certain organochlorines with good results. In 1976, for example, Congress ordered that the manufacture of polychlorinated biphenyls (PCBs) in the United States stop completely by January 1, 1979. Similarly, the organochlorine pesticide DDT—which is currently found on forty-four of the worst hazardous waste sites in the country—was banned for most uses in 1972. In both cases, because industries had no other choice, substitutes were found to replace these chemicals.

Judging from these past experiences, those in favor of sunsetting organochlorines believe that companies can adjust to the change, given the right conditions. The IJC, for example, has not recommended a sudden halt to the use of all organochlorines. Rather, it has called for the government to work with industries in setting reasonable deadlines which industries could meet, a process that would allow the industries significant input. The IJC and other proponents of sunsetting believe strongly that it is time to start setting those deadlines, however, so that these chemicals can be phased out as quickly as possible.

The IJC, the American Public Health Association, Greenpeace, and other environmental groups, though, have so far been unsuccessful in their efforts. Siding with industry on the matter, both the EPA and Canada's equivalent governmental body, Environment Canada, have refused to

*The buildup of hazardous waste has spurred many individuals to join the environmental activism effort.*

adopt recommendations to put a slow end to the use of organochlorines. However, the pressure from environmental groups has caused companies to investigate alternative methods on their own. For example, a company called Flexsys, formed through the cooperation of the Monsanto Chemical Company and Akzo Nobel, has recently found a way to eliminate the use of chlorine during the production of a chemical compound associated with the manufacture of rubber. According to the EPA, Flexsys developed this new, alternative process because "the use of chlorine . . . has come under intense scrutiny."[61]

## Individuals have affected the hazardous waste problem through activism

Although many of the decisions which lead to the reduction and elimination of hazardous waste appear at first to fall to government bodies and industry groups, ordinary people have played a central role in efforts to reduce and eliminate hazardous waste. Individuals have organized into neighborhood groups everywhere across the nation, protesting against irresponsible industries and working with cooperative local industries to prevent pollution.

To aid local organizations in their efforts, the EPA annually releases information on the amount of toxic waste generated by each large industrial facility in the country in a document called the "Toxics Release Inventory" (TRI). The TRI's purpose is to educate ordinary people about just how much toxic waste each facility near them produces. Discussing TRI in an environmental fact sheet for the public, the EPA explains: "People have a right to know what substances companies produce and discharge into their environment. TRI acts as a tool communities can use to discover types and amounts of toxic chemicals released in or near their neighborhoods. If citizens object to chemical releases in their area, they can pressure facilities to use pollution prevention and source reduction techniques to decrease releases."[62]

The environmental activism described by the EPA in its literature is a difficult and challenging activity. Asked about taking on such a role in the community, environmental activist Lois Gibbs recently explained, "When I first started . . . I felt like I didn't have enough education or wasn't qualified enough as an organizer to be the leader of the movement. . . . People have to learn, like I did, that anyone can be an activist, anyone can be a leader if they want to step forward, and when people get together they can change things."[63]

Since industrial facilities generate the vast majority of hazardous waste across the country, people who have chosen to protest against the industries that generate hazardous waste in their communities have had the greatest impact on the hazardous waste problem. However, there are other ways in which individuals have helped to reduce the creation of hazardous waste. People have made a difference, for example, by purchasing "green" products—manufactured by companies that use alternative production methods—and by choosing to purchase fewer products overall. People have also made a difference by carefully disposing of household products that qualify as hazardous waste. Batteries, paint, varnishes, chemical products, personal computers, florescent lightbulbs, mercury thermometers, and automobile products such as oil all contain hazardous chemicals and ideally should be brought to special hazardous waste dumps, or, in the case of oil, to gasoline stations that have special used-oil tanks. Many towns and cities now have one or two days of the year set aside for hazardous waste collection from the public.

## The generation of hazardous waste continues today

More than twenty years after the people of the United States awoke to the problem of hazardous waste—and more than fifty years after scientists and engineers first identified the problem—hazardous waste continues to pose a grave threat to the American environment and to the health of those exposed to wastes. Billions of dollars have been spent in a effort to clean up this contamination, but hazardous waste sites are so numerous that they threaten to overwhelm any efforts at total cleanup. Only a small fraction of sites have been decontaminated over the past twenty years.

*Workers process hazardous household waste at a collection site. Responsible disposal of dangerous household products can help reduce the hazardous waste problem.*

Meanwhile, industries, the military, and other government bodies continue to generate a vast quantity of hazardous waste every year, and the creation of hazardous waste is once again on the rise. Although waste is currently disposed of with much more caution than in previous decades, it is still released into rivers and lakes, buried in the ground in landfills that cannot last forever, and incinerated—sending toxins into the air.

People everywhere in the United States are persevering in the face of this contamination, fighting to get something done about the hazardous waste in their communities, and learning the hard way that hazardous waste contamination is a grave problem without simple solutions. Meanwhile, environmentalists look forward to a day when industrial practices change and people no longer have to struggle to live in a clean environment.

# Notes

---

### *Introduction*

1. *Online Newshour*, "Fighting Back," transcript, June 21, 1999. Available from www.pbs.org/newshour/bb/environment /jan-june99/epa_6.21.html.

2. Phil Brown and Edwin J. Mikkelsen, *No Safe Place*. Berkeley, CA: University of California Press, 1990, 1997, p. 3.

### *Chapter 1: The Hazardous Waste Problem*

3. State House News Service, "Activists Try to Shine Spotlight on Toxics Usage," *The Cambridge TAB*, April 27–May 3, 1999, p. 22.

4. State House News Service, "Activists Try to Shine Spotlight on Toxics Usage," p. 23.

5. The World Bank Group, "World Resources 1994–95: A Guide to the Global Environment, People and the Environment: Chapter 12," World Resources Institute, 1994. Available from www.worldbank.org/nipr/work_paper/wri.

6. Sandra Chereb, "Superfund May Be Used to Clean Up Sierra Mine," *Las Vegas Review-Journal*, October 22, 1999, p. 32A.

7. Quoted in Brown and Mikkelsen, *No Safe Place*, p. 129.

8. Ronald Brownstein, Ralph Nader, and John Richard, eds., *Who's Poisoning America?* San Francisco, CA: Sierra Club Books, 1981, p. 175.

9. National Institute of Environmental Health Services (NIEHS), "The Persistence of Polychlorinated Biphenyls in Hudson River Sediments," Fate and Transport Research Highlights: 1997–1998, NIEHS Superfund Basic Research Program.

### *Chapter 2: The Disposal of Hazardous Wastes and the Law*

10. Quoted in Halina Szejnwald Brown, Brian J. Cook, Robert Krueger, and Jo Anne Shatkin, "Reassessing the History of U.S. Hazardous Waste Disposal Policy—Problem Definition, Expert Knowledge and Agenda-Setting," *RISK: Health, Safety, & Environment*, Franklin Pierce Law Center, Volume 8, 1997. Available from the Franklin Pierce Law Center online at www.fplc.edu/RISK/vol8/summer/brown+. htm. p. 249.

11. Quoted in Brown, Cook, Krueger, and Shatkin, "Reassessing the History of U.S. Hazardous Waste Disposal Policy—Problem Definition, Expert Knowledge and Agenda-Setting," p. 249.

12. John G. Sprankling and Gregory S. Weber, *The Law of Hazardous Wastes and Toxic Substances*. St. Paul, MN: West Publishing Co., 1997, p. 258.

13. Jennifer Seymour Whitaker, *Salvaging the Land of Plenty*. New York: William Morrow, 1994, p. 148.

14. Environmental Protection Agency, "Regulatory Determination for Oil and Gas and Geothermal Exploration, Development and Production Wastes," July 6, 1988. Section I. Available from www.epa.gov/epaoswer/other/oil/ogreg 88.txt.

15. Environmental Defense, "Protecting People from Hazardous Wastes," website literature, 1997. Available from www.edf.org/issues/hazardouswaste.html.

16. Associated Press, "Senate Votes Against Oil Field Waste Change," *The Advocate*, Baton Rouge, LA, May 19, 1999, p. 7A. Also available from www.theadvocate.com/news/story. asp?storyid=6532.

17. James Ridgeway and Jeffrey St. Clair, *A Pocket Guide to Environmental Bad Guys*. New York: Thunder's Mouth Press, 1998, p. 94.

18. Quoted in Steve Lerner, *Eco-Pioneers*. Cambridge, MA: MIT Press, 1997, p. 326.

19. Jonathan S. Petrikin, ed., *At Issue: Environmental Justice*. San Diego, CA: Greenhaven Press, 1995, p. 10.

20. Sierra Club, "Toxics: Environment Justice." Available from www.sierraclub.org/toxics/ejhome.asp.

21. Robert Bullard, ed., *Unequal Protection*. San Francisco, CA: Sierra Club Books, 1994, pp. 4–5

22. Quoted in Stephen Braun, "Washington Neighborhood Searches for Toxics from WWI Homes Built on Field Used for Testing of Chemical Weapons," *San Francisco Chronicle*, August 31, 1999.

### *Chapter 3: Cleaning Up Hazardous Waste*

23. Quoted in Suzanne Ledel, "Lois Gibbs: Legendary Environmental Activist," *Cleveland Free Times*, December 1–7, 1999. Available from www.freetimes.com/issues/811/news-editorial.php3.

24. Philip Shabecoff, *A Fierce Green Fire*. New York: Farrar Strauss & Giroux, 1993, p. 212.

25. House Transportation and Infrastructure Committee Water Resources and Environment Subcommittee, "Statement of Carol M. Browner Administrator U.S. Environmental Protection Agency Before the Subcommittee on Water Resources and Environment U.S House of Representatives," May 12, 1999. Available from www.epa.gov/superfund/new/congress/05-12-99.htm.

26. Judith Kohler, "EPA Investigates Superfund 'Hot Rocks,'" *Fresno Bee*, September 22, 1999, p. A5.

27. Kohler, "EPA Investigates Superfund 'Hot Rocks.'" See also SC&A, Inc., "Final Report: Five-Year Review Report," in response to EPA Contract Number 68-D7-0001, November 12, 1999. Available from www.epa.gov/region08/info/polit/shattuck/Background/5yrreview.pdf.

28. Quoted in *Online Newshour*, "Paying for the Past," transcript, April 16, 1996. Available from www.pbs.org/newshour/bb/environment/superfund_4-16.html.

29. Quoted in Brownstein, Nader, and Richard, *Who's Poisoning America?* p. 334.

30. House Commerce Committee Subcommittee on Finance and Hazardous Waste, "Federal Barriers to Environmental

Cleanups," testimony of James D. Donohoe on behalf of the Ohio Steel Industry Advisory Council, Columbus, OH: February 14, 1997, p. 2.

31. Quoted in Lerner, *Eco-Pioneers*, p. 334.

32. Quoted in Lerner, *Eco-Pioneers*, p. 330.

33. Quoted in Lerner, *Eco-Pioneers*, p. 300.

34. General Accounting Office, "Hazardous Waste Sites: State Cleanup Practices," report to the Chairman, Committee on the Budget, House of Representatives, GAO/RCED-99-39, December 1998, p. 12.

35. Environmental Protection Agency, "Statement by Adm. Carol M. Browner on Superfund Markup," press release, October 1, 1999. Available from www.dakotacg.com/releases/pa/oct99/hq1004a.htm.

### *Chapter 4: Radioactive Waste*

36. *Online Newshour*, "Toxic Leaks," transcript, March 30, 1998. Available from www.pbs.org/newshour/bb/environment/jan-june98/toxic_3-30.html.

37. General Accounting Office, "Nuclear Waste: Department of Energy's Hanford Tank Waste Project—Schedule, Cost, and Management Issues," report to congressional requesters, GAO/RCED-99-13, October 1998, pp. 1, 17.

38. Michael B. Gerrard, *Whose Backyard, Whose Risk*. Cambridge, MA: MIT Press, 1994, p. 35.

39. Quoted in Ridgeway and St. Clair, *A Pocket Guide to Environmental Bad Guys*, p. 101.

40. Quoted in Nuclear Files Archive, "Dwight D. Eisenhower's 'Atoms for Peace' Address to the U.N. General Assembly, December 8, 1953." Nuclear Files Archive, Nuclear Age Peace Foundation. Available from www.nuclearfiles.org/docs/1953/531208-ike-afp.html.

41. Quoted in Arjun Makhijani, "The Nuclear Power Deception: Preface," Institute for Energy and Environmental Research (IEER), 1996. Available from www.ieer.org/reports/npd.html. See also Lewis L. Strauss, Chairman, U.S. Atomic Energy Commission, "Remarks Prepared for Delivery at the

Founders' Day Dinner, National Association of Science Writers," September 16, 1954.

42. State of Nevada, "Summary of Yucca Mountain Oversight and Impact Assessment Findings," Agency for Nuclear Projects, January 1997. Available from www.state.nv.us/nucwaste/yucca/ymsum01.htm.

43. Quoted in Jon Christensen, "New Questions Plague Nuclear Waste Storage Plan," *New York Times*, August 10, 1999, p. F1 (F4).

44. Quoted in Christensen, "New Questions Plague Nuclear Waste Storage Plan," p. F1 (F4).

45. Christensen, "New Questions Plague Nuclear Waste Storage Plan," p. F1 (F4).

46. Department of Energy, "Vision 2010," East Tennessee Technology Park, Oakridge Operations. Available at www.oakridge.doe.gov/ettp/vision.html.

47. Nuclear Information & Resource Service, "Statement to the Nuclear Regulatory Commission Opposing Atomic Waste Release/Clearance/Recycling into the Marketplace," 1999. Available from www.nirs.org/recycle/NRCGrpsStatement3.htm.

48. Quoted in Erin McCormick, "NRC Ponders Consumer Products Made of Radioactive Scrap Metal," *San Francisco Examiner*, September 19, 1999, p. A1 (A14).

49. Quoted in McCormick, "NRC Ponders Consumer Products Made of Radioactive Scrap Metal," p. A1 (A14).

50. Nuclear Information & Resource Service, "Statement to the Nuclear Regulatory Commission Opposing Atomic Waste Release/Clearance/Recycling into the Marketplace."

51. Public Citizen, "The Floodgates Are Opening for Radioactive Metal Recycling!" Critical Mass Energy Project. Available from www.citizen.org/cmep/radmetal/radrecycle.html.

### Chapter 5: Incineration, Recycling, and Reduction

52. Gerrard, *Whose Backyard, Whose Risk*, p. 115.

53. Duff Wilson, "Fear in the Fields: Part 2, How Hazardous Waste Becomes Fertilizer," *Seattle Times*, July 4, 1997.

54. Environmental Working Group, "Toxic Waste Widespread in Calif. Farm & Home Fertilizers," Press Release, November 18, 1999. Available from www.ewg.org/pub/home/Reports/AsYouSow/fertilizerpr.html.

55. Jane Kay, "Toxic Fertilizers Going Unregulated by State," *San Francisco Examiner*, November 18, 1999, p. A9.

56. William C. Blackman Jr., *Basic Hazardous Waste Management*. Boca Raton, FL: Lewis Publishers, 1993, pp. 169–70.

57. Quoted in Blackman, *Basic Hazardous Waste Management*, p. 178.

58. Gordon K. Durnil, *The Making of a Conservative Environmentalist*. Bloomington, IN: Indiana University Press, 1995, pp. 26–7.

59. American Public Health Association, "American Public Health Association Resolution 9304: Recognizing and Addressing the Environmental and Occupational Health Problems Posed by Chlorinated Organic Chemicals." American Journal of Public Health, vol. 84, no. 3, pp. 514–15.

60. Quoted in Theodore D. Goldfarb, ed., *Taking Sides: Clashing Views on Controversial Environmental Issues*. Guilford, CT: Dushkin/McGraw-Hill, 1997, p. 134.

61. Environment Protection Agency, "Presidential Green Chemistry Challenge: 1998 Alternative Synthetic Pathways Award," Office of Pollution Prevention and Toxics, 1998. Available from www.epa.gov/opptintr/greenchemistry/aspa98.htm.

62. Environmental Protection Agency, "Environmental Fact Sheet: Toxics Release Inventory Questions & Answers," Office of Communication and Public Involvement (OCPI), May 20, 1997. Available from www.epa.gov/unix0008/news/news9697/triqa97.html.

63. Quoted in Ledel, "Lois Gibbs: Legendary Environmental Activist."

# Organizations
# to Contact

**Agency for Toxic Substances and Disease Registry (ATSDR)**
1600 Clifton Rd.
Atlanta, GA 30333
(888) 422-8737
www.atsdr.cdc.gov

The Agency for Toxic Substances is responsible for preventing public exposure to contamination from hazardous waste sites, accidental chemical releases, and from other sources of pollution. ATSDR regularly assesses the contamination on hazardous waste sites, publishes fact sheets with information about the effects of exposure to toxic waste, and supports research into public health issues associated with hazardous wastes. ATSDR is an agency of the U.S. Department of Health and Human Services

**American Chemical Society (ACS)**
1155 16th St. NW
Washington, DC 20036
(202) 872-4600
www.acs.org

The American Chemical Society hopes to promote public understanding of chemistry through outreach programs. ACS also sponsors development programs and courses for chemists, chemical engineers, and technicians. Sixty percent of ACS's 161,000 members come from the world of private industry.

**American Nuclear Society (ANS)**
555 North Kensington Ave.
LaGrange Park, IL 60526
(708) 352-0499
www.ans.org

Founded in December 11, 1954, the American Nuclear Society is a not-for-profit group of engineers, scientists, and others from the nuclear industry, government agencies, and educational institutions. The ANS boasts 11,000 members. The ANS has argued, among other things, that exposure to very low levels of radiation is not only safe but possibly beneficial.

## Center for Health, Environment and Justice (CHEJ)
Formerly Citizens Clearinghouse for Hazardous Waste
150 S. Washington, Suite 300 (P.O. Box 6806)
Falls Church, VA 22040
(703) 237-2249
www.chej.org

Founded in 1981 by Lois Gibbs, the leader of residents at Love Canal, the Center for Health, Environment and Justice (CHEJ) is a grassroots organization devoted to protecting public health and the environment. CHEJ offers aid, advice, and training to neighborhood groups fighting against hazardous waste contamination in their communities.

## Department of Energy (DOE)
U.S. Department of Energy, Headquarters
Forrestal Building
1000 Independence Ave. SW
Washington, DC 20585
(202) 586-5000
www.doe.gov

The Department of Energy (DOE) is the government agency responsible for overseeing the nation's production of nuclear weapons. It also addresses energy security issues, environmental quality issues, and sponsors scientific research. The DOE has a controversial record of nuclear waste management. Under its leadership, many of the facilities involved in the production of nuclear weapons have improperly disposed of radioactive waste, leading to the contamination of facility grounds and the surrounding areas.

## Environmental Defense
Formerly Environmental Defense Fund (EDF)
Environmental Defense National Headquarters

257 Park Ave. South
New York, NY 10010
(212) 505-2100
www.edf.org

Environmental Defense, formerly known as the Environmental Defense Fund, was founded in 1967 by environmentalists in New York who worked to ban the use of the pesticide DDT. Environmental Defense addresses environmental issues through legal avenues, public education, scientific work, and political lobbying, and by working with grassroots organizations at the local level. Environmental Defense has been particularly concerned with the Bevill Amendment, which exempts certain hazardous wastes from hazardous waste regulation.

### Environmental Protection Agency (EPA)

Ariel Rios Building
1200 Pennsylvania Ave. NW
Washington, DC 20460
(202) 260-2090
www.epa.gov

The Environmental Protection Agency is the government agency charged with the protection of human health and the American environment. The EPA implements and enforces the Superfund hazardous waste site cleanup program, the Resource Conservation and Recovery Act (RCRA), the Clean Water Act, the Clean Air Act, and other federal environmental laws. The EPA also annually publishes the Toxics Release Inventory, which provides statistics on the amount of toxic waste generated in the United States, the industries generating this waste, and the manner in which this waste is disposed.

### Greenpeace

1436 U St. NW
Washington, DC 20009
(800) 326-0959
www.greenpeaceusa.org

Greenpeace started in 1971 by activists protesting the U.S. government's testing of nuclear weapons on the Pacific island of Amchitka. Greenpeace today is an international organization that uses nonviolent confrontation to further environmental causes. Among other issues, Greenpeace has focused on the disturbing trend of developed countries shipping their hazardous wastes to developing countries—where there is less regulation on the disposal of these wastes.

**Nuclear Information & Resource Service (NIRS)**
1424 16th St. NW, #404
Washington, DC 20036
(202) 328-0002
www.nirs.org

The Nuclear Information & Resource Service was founded in 1978 to provide a networking center for citizens and activists concerned with nuclear power, radioactive waste, radiation, and sustainable energy issues. The NIRS offers technical support to grassroots environmental groups involved with the issues of nuclear power, and organizes public education campaigns around issues related to the nuclear power and nuclear weapons industries. NIRS opposes the recycling of radioactive waste into consumer goods.

**Public Citizen**
1600 20th St. NW
Washington, DC 20009
(800) 289-3787
www.citizen.org

Public Citizen is a citizen group concerned with issues of public health, public safety, the environment, and consumer rights. Public Citizen is particularly focused on the problem of corporate money in politics, and is fighting to give a voice to ordinary citizens in the United States. Public Citizen was founded by Ralph Nader in 1971.

**Sierra Club**
85 Second St., Second Fl.
San Francisco, CA 94105-3441
(415) 977-5500
www.sierraclub.org

The Sierra Club began more than a century ago in 1892. The Sierra Club works to preserve and promote the responsible use of natural resources. Among other publications, this organization publishes *The Sierra Club Guide to Safe Drinking Water*, a book which looks at common forms of tap water pollution and offers information on water filters available to the public.

## U.S. General Accounting Office (GAO)

441 G St. NW
Washington, DC 20548
(202) 512-4292
www.gao.gov

The General Accounting Office (GAO) evaluates government programs to ensure that government offices remain accountable to the American people. In particular, the GAO offers a wide range of documents investigating government agencies and their role in hazardous waste management. GAO documents include analyses of state cleanup practices, cleanup at the Hanford Nuclear Reservation, and Superfund's financial status. A list of these documents is available at www.gao.gov. The documents can also be ordered by calling (202) 512-6000.

## U.S. Nuclear Regulatory Commission (NRC)

One White Flint North
11555 Rockville Pike
Rockville, MD 20852-2738
(800) 368-5642
www.nrc.gov

The U.S. Nuclear Regulatory Commission (NRC) was established by Congress in 1974 to address issues raised by the use of nuclear materials. The NRC is responsible for protecting public health and the environment in regard to the operation of nuclear power plants, the manufacture of nuclear weapons, and other activities which involve radioactive substances. The NRC is currently allowing the recycling of radioactive scrap metal into consumer goods on a case-by-case basis.

# Suggestions for Further Reading

Tricia Andryszewski, *What to Do About Nuclear Waste*. Brookfield, CT: Millbrook Press, 1995. An informative look at the issues surrounding radioactive waste. Includes chapters on nuclear weapons, nuclear power, plutonium, and the international issues raised by radioactive waste.

Lois Marie Gibbs and Murray Levine, *Love Canal: My Story*. Albany, NY: State University of New York Press, Albany, 1982. A gripping, first-hand account of the events at Love Canal in Niagara Falls, New York, where Lois Gibbs and her neighbors fought against the hazardous waste contamination that threatened their health and well-being.

Scott Alan Lewis, *The Sierra Club Guide to Safe Drinking Water*. San Francisco, CA: Sierra Club Books, 1996. Describes the contaminants most likely to be found in tap water and examines the water filters available to the public in light of these contaminants. Includes information on how to find out more about tap water contamination in specific towns and cities in the United States.

Seth Shulman, *The Threat at Home: Confronting the Toxic Legacy of the U.S. Military*. Boston, MA: Beacon Press, 1992. A telling overview of the military's management of hazardous waste over the years. Journalist Shulman looks into the problems of unexploded ordinance, groundwater contamination at military bases, and radioactive waste contamination, among other issues.

# Works Consulted

## Books

William C. Blackman Jr., *Basic Hazardous Waste Management*. Boca Raton, FL: Lewis Publishers, 1993. An introduction to hazardous waste management, written primarily for students of environmental engineering.

Phil Brown and Edwin J. Mikkelsen, *No Safe Place*. Berkeley, CA: University of California Press, 1990, 1997. A carefully researched examination of the problems which people face linking abnormal instances of illness in a community to hazardous waste contamination.

Ronald Brownstein, Ralph Nader, and John Richard, eds., *Who's Poisoning America*? San Francisco, CA: Sierra Club Books, 1981. Offers essays on toxic waste contamination across the United States, written at a time when the hazardous waste contamination in Niagara Falls, New York, had focused the public's attention on the issue.

Robert Bullard, ed., *Unequal Protection*. San Francisco, CA: Sierra Club Books, 1994. A collection of essays concerning the issue of environmental justice, edited by one of the leaders of the environmental justice movement.

Gordon K. Durnil, *The Making of a Conservative Environmentalist*. Bloomington, IN: Indiana University Press, 1995. Written by Republican politician Gordon K. Durnil, this book argues that conservatives in the United States need to take a more active environmental role. Durnil researched the problem of pollution in the Great Lakes while acting as chairman of the International Joint Commission—a binational governmental body responsible for addressing issues concerning surface waters which border the United States and Canada.

Michael B. Gerrard, *Whose Backyard, Whose Risk.* Cambridge, MA: MIT Press, 1994. Environmental lawyer Michael Gerrard offers an exhaustive and well-researched account of the problems surrounding the siting of disposal facilities for hazardous waste and radioactive wastes.

Theodore D. Goldfarb, ed., *Taking Sides: Clashing Views on Controversial Environmental Issues.* Guilford, CT: Dushkin/McGraw-Hill, 1997. A collection of writings on the environment with opposing viewpoints offered on each issue, followed by a thoughtful afterword in each section by the editor.

Michael I. Greenberg, Richard J. Hamilton and Scott D. Phillips, eds., *Occupational, Industrial, and Environmental Toxicology.* St. Louis, MO: Mosby, 1997. A reference book offering basic information on the hazards which workers face in a wide variety of industries.

Steve Lerner, *Eco-Pioneers.* Cambridge, MA: MIT Press, 1997. Each chapter in this book offers an account of a positive environmental trend or technology.

Raymond L. Murray, *Understanding Radioactive Waste.* Columbus, OH: Battelle Press, 1994. Provides a detailed introduction to radioactive waste, with a focus on scientific issues rather than political or sociological ones.

Organization for Economic Co-operation and Development (OECD), *OECD Proceedings: Sources of Cadmium in the Environment.* Paris, France: OECD, 1996. Offers a series of papers presented at an international conference concerned with cadmium pollution.

Jonathan S. Petrikin, ed., *At Issue: Environmental Justice.* San Diego, CA: Greenhaven Press, 1995. Includes essays and articles on the issue of environmental justice, ranging from fact-based discussions of the issue to personal viewpoint editorials.

James Ridgeway and Jeffrey St. Clair, *A Pocket Guide to Environmental Bad Guys.* New York: Thunder's Mouth

Press, 1998. A pocket book which briefly covers some of the environmental issues facing the United States today, with a focus on the role that individuals and companies have played in environmental problems.

Fred Setterberg and Lonny Shavelson, *Toxic Nation*. New York: John Wiley & Sons, Inc., 1993. Writer Setterberg and photographer Shavelson traveled across the United States, interviewing people who have fought against pollution in their communities. This book recounts individual struggles in an effort to show the breadth of environmental problems facing Americans.

Philip Shabecoff, *A Fierce Green Fire*. New York: Farrar Straus & Giroux, 1993. Written by *New York Times* reporter Philip Shabecoff, this book provides a well-researched account of the environmental issues which Shabecoff covered over several decades.

K. S. Shrader-Frechette, *Burying Uncertainty*. Berkeley, CA: University of California Press, 1993. Scientist Shrader-Frechette examines the issue of placing radioactive waste in Yucca Mountain, Nevada, with an emphasis on the difficulties of predicting geological events and the assumptions underlying scientific research on the geology of Yucca Mountain.

John G. Sprankling and Gregory S. Weber, *The Law of Hazardous Wastes and Toxic Substances*. St. Paul, MN: West Publishing Co., 1997. An introduction to major environmental laws, including the Superfund law and the Resource Conservation and Recovery Act (RCRA).

Jennifer Seymour Whitaker, *Salvaging the Land of Plenty*. New York: William Morrow, 1994. Written for a popular audience, this book takes a look at the issue of waste in the United States and the environmental challenges facing the country for the future.

### *Periodicals*

Adrianne Appel, "Toxic site cleanups are at risk," *Boston Globe*, July 5, 1999.

American Public Health Association, "American Public Health Association Resolution 9304: Recognizing and Addressing the Environmental and Occupational Health Problems Posed by Chlorinated Organic Chemicals." American Journal of Public Health, vol. 84, no. 3.

Associated Press, "Senate Votes Against Oil Field Waste Change," *The Advocate*, Baton Rouge, LA, May 19: 1999.

Stephen Braun, "Washington Neighborhood Searches for Toxics from WWI Homes Built on Field Used for Testing of Chemical Weapons," *San Francisco Chronicle*, August 31, 1999.

Halina Szejnwald Brown, Brian J. Cook, Robert Krueger, and Jo Anne Shatkin, "Reassessing the History of U.S. Hazardous Waste Disposal Policy—Problem Definition, Expert Knowledge and Agenda-Setting," *RISK: Health, Safety, & Environment*, Franklin Pierce Law Center, Volume 8, 1997. www.fplc.edu/RISK/vol8/summer/brownt.htm.

Jon Christensen, "New Questions Plague Nuclear Waste Storage Plan," *New York Times*, August 10, 1999.

Sandra Chereb, "Superfund May Be Used to Clean Up Sierra Mine," *Las Vegas Review-Journal*, October 22, 1999.

Committee to Bridge the Gap, Letter to Dr. Rick Jostes, Study Director of BEIR VII at the National Research Council, June 22, 1999. This letter is available upon request from Dan Hirsch, Executive Director, Committee to Bridge the Gap, (831) 462-6136.

General Accounting Office, "Hazardous Waste Sites: State Cleanup Practices," report to the Chairman, Committee on the Budget, House of Representatives, GAO/RCED-99-39, December 1998.

General Accounting Office, "Nuclear Waste: Department of Energy's Hanford Tank Waste Project—Schedule, Cost, and Management Issues," report to congressional requesters, GAO/RCED-99-13, October 1998.

House Commerce Committee Subcommittee on Finance and Hazardous Waste, "Federal Barriers to Environmental

Cleanups," testimony of James D. Donohoe on behalf of the Ohio Steel Industry Advisory Council, Columbus, OH: February 14, 1997.

Jane Kay, "Toxic Fertilizers Going Unregulated by State," *San Francisco Examiner*, November 18, 1999.

Judith Kohler, "EPA Investigates Superfund 'Hot Rocks,'" *Fresno Bee*, September 22, 1999.

Suzanne Ledel, "Lois Gibbs: Legendary Environmental Activist," *Cleveland Free Times,* December 1–7, 1999. www.freetimes.com/issues/811/news-editorial.php3.

Erin McCormick, "NRC Ponders Consumer Products Made of Radioactive Scrap Metal," *San Francisco Examiner*, September 19, 1999.

National Institute of Environmental Health Services (NIEHS), "The Persistence of Polychlorinated Biphenyls in Hudson River Sediments," Fate and Transport Research Highlights: 1997–1998, NIEHS Superfund Basic Research Program.

State House News Service, "Activists Try to Shine Spotlight on Toxics Usage," *The Cambridge TAB*, April 27–May 3, 1999.

Matthew L. Wald, "Study Advances Plan for Nuclear Storage Site, but Questions Remain," *New York Times*, August 7, 1999.

Joby Warrick, "In Harm's Way, And in the Dark," *Washington Post*, August 8, 1999.

Duff Wilson, "Fear in the Fields: Part 2, How Hazardous Waste Becomes Fertilizer," *Seattle Times*, July 4, 1997.

### *Internet Sources*

Agency for Toxic Substances and Disease Registry, "Minimal Risk Levels (MRLs) for Hazardous Substances," Division of Toxicology. www.atsdr.cdc.gov/mrls.html.

Agency for Toxic Substances and Disease Registry, "ToxFAQs." www.atsdr.cdc.gov/toxfaq.html.

American Nuclear Society, "Health Effects of Low-Level Radiation," Position Statement, April 1999. www.ans.org/PI/lowlevel.html.

CNN.com, "Clinton: Companies Must Make Chemical Use Public," October 30, 1999. www.cnn.com/ALLPOLITICS/stories/1999/10/30/clinton.radio/index.html.

Department of Energy, "Vision 2010," East Tennessee Technology Park, Oakridge Operations. www.oakridge.doe.gov/ettp/vision.html.

Environmental Defense, "Protecting People from Hazardous Wastes," website literature, 1997. www.edf.org/issues/hazardouswaste.html.

Environmental Protection Agency, "1997 Toxics Release Inventory: Public Data Release Report," April 1999. www.epa.gov/tri/tri97/pdr/index.htm.

Environmental Protection Agency, "About Environmental Justice," Office of Solid Waste and Emergency Response. www.epa.gov/swerosps/ej/aboutej.htm.

Environmental Protection Agency, "Chemical Summary for Perchloroethylene," Office of Pollution Prevention and Toxics, August 1994. www.epa.gov/opptintr/chemfact/s_perchl.txt.

Environmental Protection Agency, "Regulatory Determination for Oil and Gas and Geothermal Exploration, Development and Production Wastes," July 6, 1988. Section I. www.epa.gov/epaoswer/other/oil/ogreg88.txt.

Environmental Protection Agency, "Statement by Carol M. Browner, Administrator on House Subcommittee Superfund Markup," Friday, October 1, 1999. www.dakotacg.com/releases/pa/oct99/hq1004a.htm.

Environmental Working Group, "Toxic Waste Widespread in Calif. Farm & Home Fertilizers," Press Release, November 18, 1999. www.ewg.org/pub/home/Reports/AsYouSow/fertilizerpr.html.

House Transportation and Infrastructure Committee Water Resources and Environment Subcommittee, "Statement of Carol M. Browner Administrator U.S. Environmental Protection Agency Before the Subcommittee on Water Resources and Environment U.S House of Representatives," May 12, 1999. www.epa.gov/superfund/new/congress/05-12-99.htm.

Arjun Makhijani, "The Nuclear Power Deception: Preface," Institute for Energy and Environmental Research (IEER), 1996. www.ieer.org/reports/npd.html.

National Safety Council, "Yucca Mountain: Frequently Asked Questions," Environmental Health Center, November 11, 1999. www.nsc.org/ehc/yucca/yuccafaq.htm.

State of Nevada, "Earthquakes Rocking Yucca Mountain Area." www.state.nv.us/nucwaste/news/quake/quake1.htm.

State of Nevada, "Summary of Yucca Mountain Oversight and Impact Assessment Findings," Agency for Nuclear Projects, January 1997. www.state.nv.us/nucwaste/yucca/ymsum01.htm.

Nuclear Files Archive, "Dwight D. Eisenhower's 'Atoms for Peace' Address to the U.N. General Assembly, December 8, 1953," Nuclear Files Archive, Nuclear Age Peace Foundation. www.nuclearfiles.org/docs/1953/531208-ike-afp.html.

Nuclear Information & Resource Service, "Energy Secretary's Action on Radioactive Metal Falls Short, Still Allows Radioactive Waste in Household Products," Press Release, January 12, 2000. www.nirs.org/recycle/pcdoerecl1122000.txt.

Nuclear Information & Resource Service, "One Hundred Eighty-Seven Organizations Call on Vice President Gore to Stop Radioactive Recycling into Consumer Products," Press Release, August 12, 1999. www.nirs.org/recycle/81299Gorecombprlt.htm.

Nuclear Information & Resource Service, "Statement to the Nuclear Regulatory Commission Opposing Atomic Waste

Release/Clearance/Recycling into the Marketplace," 1999.
www.nirs.org/recycle/NRCGrpsStatement3.htm.

*Online Newshour*, "Fighting Back," transcript, June 21,
1999. www.pbs.org/newshour/bb/environment/jan-
june99/epa_6.21.html.

*Online Newshour*, "Paying for the Past," transcript, April 16,
1996. www.pbs.org/newshour/bb/environment/superfund_4-
16.html.

*Online Newshour*, "Toxic Leaks," transcript, March 30, 1998.
www.pbs.org/newshour/bb/environment/jan-june98/toxic_3-
30.html.

Public Citizen, "The Floodgates Are Opening for
Radioactive Metal Recycling!" Critical Mass Energy
Project. www.citizen.org/cmep/radmetal/radrecycle.html.

Public Citizen, "Nuclear Waste Fact Sheet," Critical Mass
Energy Project, January 6, 2000. www.citizen.org/cmep/RAGE/
radwaste/Nukewstfactsht.htm.

Right-To-Know Network, "Facility Report (BRS Data); Facility:
GE Plastics-Selkirk Operation," Copy of Environmental
Protection Agency's BRS database, EPA ID NYD066832023,
Reporting Year 1995. www.rtk.net/ix-bin/brs/nph-
cgibrs_f?FACILITY_NAME_1=&CITY=&STATE=ALL+--
+Entire+U.S.&REPORTING_YEAR=1995&FACILITY_ID
=NYD066832023&DETAIL=H+High&DATYPE=T+Text&
EMAIL=&ESUBJ= (visit http://db.rtk.net for more
information).

SC&A, Inc., "Final Report: Five-Year Review Report," in
response to EPA Contract Number 68-D7-0001, November
12, 1999. www.epa.gov/region08/info/polit/shattuck/
Background/5yrreview.pdf.

Sierra Club, "Toxics: Environment Justice."
www.sierraclub.org/toxics/ejhome.asp.

The World Bank Group, "World Resources 1994–95: A
Guide to the Global Environment, People and the

Environment: Chapter 12," World Resources Institute, 1994.
www.worldbank.org/nipr/work_paper/wri.

### *Legal Cases*

*United States v. Conservation Chemical Co.*, 619 F. Supp.
162 (1985).

### *Talks*

Paul Gunter, "The Future of Nuclear Power: Revitalized or
Moribund," Talk sponsored by Share A Vital Earth (SAVE),
Conducted at the Massachusetts Institute of Technology
(MIT), November 8, 1999.

# Index

# Picture Credits

Cover photo: © Tony Stone Images/Michael Rosenfield
AP Photo, 64
AP Photo/Mike Derer, 21
AP Photo/Don Heupel, 41
AP Photo/Nevada Appeal/Rick Gunn/File, 65
AP Photo/Carlos Osorio, 52
AP Photo/Douglas C. Pizac, 30
AP Photo/Reed Saxon, 79
AP Photo/David Zalubowski, 47, 59
CNP/Ron Sachs/Archive Photos, 45
© K. Condyles/Impact Visuals, 36, 51
© Natalie Fobes/Corbis, 19
© Kathleen Foster/Impact Visuals, 42
© Philip Gould/Corbis, 33
© Robert Maass/Corbis, 80
© David Maung/Impact Visuals, 56
PhotoDisc, 7, 13, 16, 22, 29, 62, 83
Reuters/Joe Traver/Archive Photos, 48
© Charles E. Rotkin/Corbis, 69
© Galen Rowell/Corbis, 43
© Joseph Sohm; ChromoSohm Inc./Corbis, 85
© Jim West/Impact Visuals, 35, 74

# About the Author

Keith McGowan is the author of *Sexual Harassment* for Lucent Books. Besides writing, he loves to travel. He has lived in Australia, Haiti, and Chile, and traveled extensively through southeast Asia and China. At present he lives in Massachusetts and is writing a science fiction story for adults.